E
F
Riviera

by

ADAM HOPKINS

Adam Hopkins is a travel writer and regular
contributor to the Sunday Times and The
Guardian. He is the author of books on
Holland and Crete.

Produced by the Publishing Division of
The Automobile Association

Written by Adam Hopkins
Peace and Quiet feature
by Paul Sterry
Consultant: Frank Dawes

Edited, designed and produced by
the Publishing Division of The
Automobile Association. Maps ©
The Automobile Association 1990.

Distributed in the United Kingdom
by the Publishing Division of The
Automobile Association, Fanum
House, Basingstoke, Hampshire,
RG21 2EA

The contents of this publication are
believed correct at the time of
printing. Nevertheless, the
publishers cannot accept
responsibility for errors or
omissions, nor for changes in details
given.

A CIP catalogue record for this book
is available from the British Library.

ISBN 0 86145 868 0

Published by The Automobile
Association

Typesetting: Microset Graphics Ltd,
Basingstoke
Colour separation: L C Repro,
Aldermaston
Printing: Printers S.R.L., Trento, Italy

*Front cover picture: Roquebrune, on
the Nice and Monte-Carlo coast*

The Automobile Association would like to
thank the following photographers and
libraries for their assistance in the
compilation of this book.

FRENCH PICTURE LIBRARY 40 Picasso
Museum, 64 Hotel Elysée Palace, Nice, 67
Modern Art Museum, 71 Monte-Carlo, 75
Océanographique Inst. Monaco, 79
Roseraire de Princess Grace, 80 Changing
the Guard at Palace, 83 Café de Paris.

A. HOPKINS 14 Painting, The Bravade, 16
Café des Arts, 17 Leather shop, 39 Le
Caveau Provençal, Cannes, 92
Villefranche.

INTERNATIONAL PHOTOBANK 4 Nice, 8
St. Tropez, 19 Artist, 22 Narrow Streets, St.
Tropez, 27 Port Grimaud, 30 St. Tropez
Restaurant, 31 Port of Cannes, 34/5 La
Croisette Beach, 43 Antibes Market, 48
Juan-Les-Pins, 55 Nice from Mont Alba, 58
Café on Castle Hill, 61 Russian Orthodox
Cathedral, 69 Café in Rue Masséna, 89
Menton, 106 Antibes, 109 Fresh Seafood,
111 Auberge Belle, 115 Menton.

NATURE PHOTOGRAPHERS LTD 93
Perfume Crop (B Burbidge), 94/5 Greilada

Elegans (P Sterry), 96/7 Greater Flamingo
(E K Thompson), 98 Little Egret, 99 Little
Bustard (K J Carlson), 100 Provence Orchid
(B Burbidge), 103 Alpine Marmots
(P Sterry), 104 Long eared bat
(O Newman), 105 Ant Lion (S C Bisserot).

BARRIE SMITH Cover Roquebrune, 13 St.
Tropez, Tahiti Plage, 21 Fréjus, Roman
Remains, 33 Cannes, Carlton Hotel, 36 Iles
St. Honorat, 44/5 Cagnes-Sur-Mer, 46
Molinard Grasse, 51 Mougins, 52 Sculpture,
Maeght Foundation, 56/7 Nice, 59 Old Nice,
84/5 Port Beaulieu, 86 Èze, 90 Menton, 108
Riviera Specialities, 113 Boules, St. Tropez,
117 Street Vendor, Nice, 118 Nice, 123
Vence, 125 Nr. St. Tropez.

SPECTRUM COLOUR LIBRARY 24/5
Grimaud Castle, 28/9 St. Raphael Beach, 72
Monaco, Casino, 76 Grottes de
l'Observatoire.

This book employs a
simple rating system to
help choose which
places to visit:

◆◆◆   do not miss

◆◆   see if you can

◆   worth seeing if
      you have time

A celebrated and glamorous coastline: the Côte d'Azur

INTRODUCTION

Everybody has heard of the French Riviera. Almost everybody has heard of the Côte d'Azur — another name for that extraordinarily famous little stretch of coast backed by mountains, washed by a warm sea, splashed by vivid sun, running from somewhere like St Tropez or St Raphael along to the Italian border. The names of the main towns are equally famous — not just St Tropez, but Nice and Cannes and Monte-Carlo, centrepiece of the tiny state of Monaco.

One reason for going to the Côte d'Azur is simply to gratify curiosity about a coastline whose name is a shorthand for luxury and glamour, for film stars and singers, politicians and millionaires. And, yes, a lot of what one hears is true. The solid wealth is amazing, the elegance is considerable, the echoes of a gorgeous past endure into a more hectic present. One visible reminder is the presence

of great hotels from the end of the last century
and the start of this; hotels whose names and
fame, as you get to know them, become a
fundamental part of the whole. Then, of course,
there is the gambling of Monte-Carlo and many
other resorts; now also equipped with casinos.
Yet the Riviera is an open place as well. Those
who are young or not well-off can also take a
share — not quite, perhaps, at the centre of
events, but near enough to get a smell of them
and understand something of the meaning of
the word 'Riviera'.

At the same time, the area has an immense
number of other points of interest and
attraction; they range from a rugged hinterland
or *arrière-pays*, whose high hill villages were
fortified positions, to some of the most
evocative, beautiful and challenging of late
19th-century works of art. Signac, Seurat,
Renoir, Bonnard, Chagall, Dufy, Léger,
Cocteau, Picasso and Matisse all lived and
painted here. The landscapes that attracted
them are often stunning; the sense of
'southernness' delightful.

A Little History

One way to get a feeling of this southern coast
of France is to take in just the briefest historical
résumé.

Parts of the coast were inhabited in prehistoric
times by cave-dwellers. As we approach
written history, the Ligurian tribespeople of this
and the north Italian coast were in possession.
Next came the Greeks. They colonised
Marseilles and then spread out to found lesser
colonies, Nice and Antibes among them. The
Romans succeeded the Greeks, leaving
substantial cities further to the west, and also
some on the Riviera. Fréjus is the main
example, though there are important Roman
remains at La Turbie on the mountain above
Monte-Carlo.

After the Romans, a moderately peaceful
experience of the so-called Dark Ages was
interrupted by the Saracens, the Mediterranean
coast's equivalent of the Vikings in northern
Europe. Saracen is a generic name for anyone
— normally Islamic — who came from North
Africa or the eastern Mediterranean and made

a nuisance of themselves to local people. After the Saracens, parts of the coast came under the control of the Counts of Provence. Other chunks were ruled by an enterprising family called Grimaldi, spreading out from Genoa to take over many lordships and still today retaining Monaco. Spaniards and other rulers came and went. The eastern part — Nice in particular — fell under the rule of Savoy and remained in effect Italian for centuries — right up to 1860 in the case of Nice.

The area also has a Napoleonic story. The young captain from Corsica made his name in the struggle for Toulon and, as his career progressed, passed frequently through on one great errand or another, including his departure into exile in Elba from St Raphael and his return via Golfe Juan in 1815.

From 30 or 40 years earlier than this, the coast

was already turning into the world's first recognisable Riviera. This fascinating process, involving the arrival of the grand and very grand to pass the winter in a milder climate, is discussed in individual entries (see Nice and Cannes in particular). The point is that the Riviera was a winter phenomenon, beginning to extend to the summer by the 1930s but not fully converted to 'sun-and-sea-and-nakedness' until after World War II. The Riviera we encounter today, bursting with crowds, its roads almost at a standstill with traffic, festive, elegant, enticing, is a modern artefact, animated by an extraordinary past.

When we stop to wonder what most precisely represents the Riviera today, one answer might be the unbelievably dense thickets of masts poking up above the sea-walls from scores of marinas all along the coast. They are a product of wealth, a symbol of the beauty of the boats beneath, a tribute to pleasure, sun and sea; and then there is all the rest.

HOW TO USE THIS GUIDE

About This Book

The Riviera is defined in this guidebook as the coast line from Le Lavandou in the southwest to Menton just on the Italian border in the east. This is a common-sense definition which sets aside a good deal of arid argument. The *arrière-pays* or hinterland immediately behind the coast is also included. For the reader's convenience, the whole area has been divided into three sections, named after the principal coastal towns or resorts. These sections are: St Tropez and the southwest coast; the Cannes coast; and the Nice and Monte-Carlo coast.

In each section the first major entry refers to the principal town or resort. The entry for each of these principal towns or resorts is made up of the following parts: Introduction; Background (usually early history); What to see (museums, churches, other notable buildings, etc); Accommodation; Nightlife; Restaurants; Shopping; Special Events.

The Principality of Monaco (including Monte-Carlo) is a separate state within the geographical borders of France.

ST TROPEZ AND THE SOUTHWEST COAST

ST TROPEZ AND THE SOUTHWEST COAST

The southwest coast of the Riviera, from Le Lavandou to Théoule by way of St Tropez, is varied and beautiful. The southernmost stretch is little spoiled and decidedly wild in places, particularly just inland in the Massif des Maures. After the peninsula of St Tropez, the coast doubles back on itself to form the Gulf of St Tropez. The extraordinary town of that name is on the southern side of the gulf; Ste Maxime on the northern side. Fréjus and St Raphael, a little further to the north again, together make up a considerable resort and town.

For over 100 years St Tropez has worked its magic on artists and writers; now film stars are among the admirers of this little town

Next, in one of the finest stretches of the whole Riviera, the road runs round the Esterel Massif. Those who go inland here will be amply rewarded.

ST TROPEZ

St Tropez, its name a by-word for extravagance of style, is the queen and concubine of its own section of the Riviera. Though not much bigger than a large village — an exceptionally lovely village — it is one of the world's hot spots for displays of fashion and fashionable behaviour. Or is it? Has it had its day? Fashion magazines and gossip columns each year debate these agonising questions. Are visitors such as Liza Minelli, Cher and Richard Chamberlain, the pundits ask, one tenth as glamorous as the likes of Brigitte Bardot and Roger Vadim, who gave the place its zest in the heady '60s? Whatever views one may have on the finer shadings of the issue, there are a number of incontrovertible facts. Sleek yachts still throng the pink and yellow waterfront, their owners conducting dinner parties and champagne receptions in full view of the crowds strolling along the quays, cameras at the ready. Meanwhile, on the other side of the road, another multitude of the elegant and the aspirant is seated at waterfront cafés whose names are almost as famous as that of St Tropez itself — Le Gorille (The Gorilla), and Sénéquier with its red awnings. Restaurants are teeming with people, and discos and nightclubs carry on the good work till dawn. If a crowd doesn't put you off, then it is entertainment indeed to join the animated throng, whether one's place is among the smart and wealthy or among the rubberneckers who have come to see them. It is a non-stop carnival. Just across the headland, on beaches with names like Tahiti Plage and Club 55, the same extravagant style finds a place among beach umbrellas and every seaside appurtenance a hedonist could wish for.

To understand the town, the lie of the land and the intimate connections of St Tropez and water, it would be best on first arrival to close one's eyes to all diversions, and climb directly to the **Citadel** above the old harbour. If the Citadel and its naval museum are closed for lunch, as they often seem to be, then the outer ramparts will be sufficient. From this vantage point the visitor looks north over the huddle of roofs and the church in the immediate foreground to the glittering blues of the Gulf of St Tropez. Sailing boats criss-cross the azure sound with a flutter of white canvas; power boats leave bright white wakes behind them in the blue; luxury yachts the size of ships, gleaming in sunlight, proceed at a more sedate pace.

On the far shores of the gulf, one can easily make out the dense scattering of houses which today form as much a part of the character of the Riviera as do the actual resorts. The Riviera is not so much built up, as well used. From St Tropez, you can see the houses climb the lower mountain slopes among the greenery and ascend right over the top of some of the hilly capes. Every now and then, the sprinkling of houses along the water-line is interrupted by the denser white mass of one of the resort towns. The summer sea, the boats at play, resorts and cubes of houses — some extremely inventive when one gets closer — all this is true Riviera and it is on display from the Citadel of St Tropez.

Painters' Light

The effect, even on those who disapprove of the density of it all, is one of light and airiness, a little like the illustrations in a cheerful children's book. The town of St Tropez itself, as one descends from the Citadel, is revealed as a delightful place, full of unexpected quirks and corners. There is no difficulty at all in understanding why, for 100 years and more, it has attracted so many marvellous painters — among them Signac, Bonnard and the great Matisse — who have duly laboured to give their canvasses the true feeling of the town.

Works by all these artists can be seen in a spacious former chapel beside the Old Harbour (see **Annonciade Museum** below). Amid the jollity and gallivanting of the present, the visitor can still feel and respond to the original azure breeziness the painters loved and tried to catch.

Most Riviera resorts face south and are in shade by late afternoon. St Tropez, unique in looking northwards across its gulf, is somewhat shadowed in the morning but catches the evening sun and basks in it. Now the façades of the harbour houses and the great white yachts across the road from them are a glorious sight, bathed in a softer, more reflective light.

To go down from the Citadel to the Old Harbour, whether at

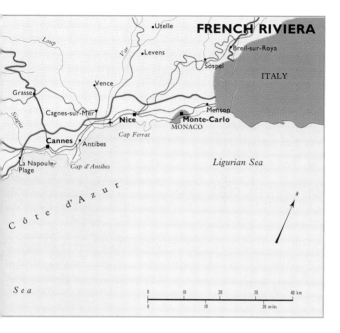

noon or nightfall, you thread
your way through narrow
streets. One way wiggles past a
fortified tower and the
handkerchief-sized pebble
beach of **la Ponche.** Here there
are two restaurants with
extremely pleasing terraces
crowded into the tiny space
available. Or you can go down
more directly, passing
multitudes of little restaurants
and smart clothes shops and the
handsome pink town hall, and
then perhaps find yourself
boxed in by an odd-shaped
little market-square, the **place
des Herbes,** with fish and
vegetables on sale. One more
wiggle and you have reached
the harbour front.

Now, after a drink at a café, one
might walk up again, taking the
tiny avenue Clémenceau to one
of the loveliest spots in St
Tropez — the **place des Lices,** a
sandy square (or rectangle)
shaded by columns of pollarded
plane trees, bounded by cafés
and restaurants, some of them
extremely famous (see
Restaurants, below). There is a
market on Saturday and
Tuesday. This used to be a
good place for spotting the
established celebrities whose
names were linked with St
Tropez from early days and who
still live locally. Nowadays, they
keep themselves increasingly to
themselves in the privacy of
their own villas. But there are
still plenty of well-known
newcomers whose pleasure it is

to see and be seen in venues like the Café des Arts here on the place des Lices or in nightspots like the Caves du Roy.

A Stylish Day

People do dress up in St Tropez and this is one of the pleasures of eating out, going on for entertainment or simply of walking in the street. The ideal way to spend a day in St Tropez might be to dress up just a little − this could involve an elegant diminution of dress rather than the addition of extras; take one's breakfast on the front at Sénéquier; proceed by push-bike, scooter, car or yacht to one's chosen beach on the far side of the headland; then, after a day of sun and sea and lunch at a beach restaurant, spent in the company of plenty of beautiful bodies, return to town for a coffee and a shower, more dressing up, a drink and then dinner, and on to whatever night-time venue one is audacious enough to try, ending up with a steak tartare at Le Gorille on the waterfront at 4am. If one doesn't have a yacht or car or elegant clothes or even any money to speak of, the spectacle is still an entertainment of considerable merit.

Visitors

St Tropez was founded by Greeks (fanning out from Marseilles) but got its name, so legend has it, from a Roman knight called Torpes. Torpes, on becoming a Christian, was beheaded by wicked Nero in faraway Italy and his decapitated body was sent forth on the Mediterranean in a boat which also contained, according to one version, a pig, a cock, a viper and a dog. This gallimaufry of animals failed to consume the body of the martyr which duly came ashore here in the bay. An evocative model in a glass case in the church shows cock and dog in a wooden boat at either end of the decapitated body. Throughout the Middle Ages St Tropez played a stout role in maritime defence and was home of the illustrious Bailli de Suffren (1792-88), celebrated for his many victories in a harbour front statue. His castle still stands in the town. A locally-produced military man, one Général Allard, after whom a street is named, served a prince in India for many years and himself married an Indian princess. This lady was in St Tropez when she heard news of the general's death in battle. She immediately converted to Christianity and lived on as a widow here for another 40 years.

Illustrious visitors began to arrive at the end of the 19th century. The writer Guy de Maupassant put St Tropez in a short story with this description: 'It is one of those charming, simple daughters of the sea, one of the modest little towns that have grown in the water like a shellfish, fed on fish and sea air, and which produces sailors. It smells of fish and burning tar, brine and boats. Sardine scales glisten like pearls on the cobblestones'.

The painter Paul Signac came here in 1892 and stayed for nearly 30 years, attracting many other artists. Henri Matisse was here in 1904 and Bonnard was a regular visitor early in this century. Before World War II the writer Colette spent months at a time in her villa in St Tropez.

The little port took on its modern style of razzmatazz and celebrity when Roger Vadim used it as the setting for the film 'And God created Woman', starring his young wife Brigitte Bardot. The film made Bardot's name and helped make St Tropez a glittering centre for personalities of cinema, the media and entertainment generally.

The Beaches

The beaches of St Tropez face southwards on the far side of the headland, 2 ½ to 3 miles (4 to 5km) from the resort, most of them backed by vines. They

The sheltered Tahiti Plage, some 2½ miles (4km) away from St Tropez, extends into Pampelonne Beach and attracts large crowds

are, in fact, one single, spectacular, sandy beach, divided into numerous private sectors replete with beach restaurants, bars, boats, water-skiing, tenders to fetch arrivals from yachts anchoring offshore and, in some cases, jacuzzis and even swimming pools. These beaches are reached by what seems at first a confusing network of lanes. Access is easiest by scooter or car but parking can be a problem — some beaches do the parking for you, New York style. All the beaches have different and sometimes contrasting characters. Some examples:

Club 55 Caters for the Paris crowd. It can take a long time to get a meal in summer; in winter there is a huge log fire in the restaurant. Open at Christmas and New Year.

Tahiti Plage The oldest beach. Sometimes seems to attract older men with younger female companions.

Blouch and Liberté Both nudist beaches.

Moorea A fun beach, relaxed with good and simple food.

Voile Rouge An adventurous crowd with extremely pretty girls and hard men from Marseilles. Mine host pours the champagne in surprising ways.

Tropezina Welcoming and sympathetic with the youngest crowd, many aged from 15 to 18.

Nioulargo The Vietnamese restaurant here has attracted many celebrities, not least the late Franz-Josef Strauss of Bavaria.

WHAT TO SEE

◆◆◆
ANNONCIADE MUSEUM,
St Tropez harbour front.
The Annonciade gallery occupies a former chapel, large and handsomely converted into a two-storey exhibition space. The gallery itself, its setting and above all the collection of paintings held there constitute one of the high spots of the Riviera. It is a celebration of the many painters who saw the beauty of St Tropez from the 1880s till about 1950, and a testimony to the depth and vision of French painting generally during these years. The period up to World War I is exceptionally well represented. The ground floor shows a number of works by Paul Signac (1863-1935), the pointilliste painter who was first to settle here and attracted many others. There are works in the same style by several of Signac's contemporaries. The picture most prominently displayed is the famous carnival view by Kees van Dongen, showing a woman in a huge black hat, arm draped round a balcony railing, smiling beside an enigmatic companion cut in half by the edge of the painting. Matisse's well-known *La Gitane* is also here. A side-gallery holds

The Bravade, *a celebration of St Torpes, is vividly depicted by artist Dany Lartigue (see p15)*

drawings and water-colours. Upstairs, the accent is on light, water and colour, with paintings of many harbours, Mediterranean and Atlantic. St Tropez itself features prominently. Bonnard, Rouault, Dufy, Vlaminck, Matisse and many others are all in top form here. There are evocative paintings of the place des Lices by Charles Camoin — and outside, through the window, the real harbour of St Tropez, source of so much inspiration. *Closed*: Tuesdays and November

◆
CHURCH OF ST TROPEZ
This neo-Baroque, 19th-century building possesses not only the model of St Torpes in his boat but also a bust of the saint which is paraded ceremonially through the streets on suitable occasions. One of these is depicted in a cheerful painting (to the left on entry) by Dany Lartigue, a St Tropez painter who proceeds about the place by bicycle with his dog in a basket.

◆
CITADEL
The handsome hexagonal keep houses St Tropez's Maritime Museum, with exhibits from early days to Allied landings in August 1944.
Closed: Thursdays and much of December

Accommodation
St Tropez has numerous hotels of all classes, some a little out of town — which could be a blessing in season. St Tropez is no place to think of starting an economy campaign, however, and even the 'cheap' hotels can hurt on the day of reckoning. Expensive hotels include:
La Bastide de St Tropez, route des Carles (tel: 94 97 58 16). Up on the slope behind the town, has a gentle Provençal elegance.
Le Byblos, ave Paul Signac (tel: 94 97 00 04). A most attractive hotel, built round courtyards and terraces, right under the Citadel of St Tropez. Very fashionable.
La Mandarine, route de Tahiti (tel: 94 97 21 00). Agreeable and peaceful setting, a little cheaper than the Byblos or Bastide de St Tropez.
Reasonable:
Hôtel de la Ponche, place du Revelin (tel: 94 97 02 53). Very pretty hotel in one of the prettiest corners of the old town.
Sube Continental, Sur le Port, reached by passage behind statue of Bailli de Suffren (tel: 94 97 30 04). Marvellous, creaking old hotel, the only one with rooms on the harbour front.
Résidence la Maison Blanche, place des Lices (tel: 94 97 52 66). Attractive residence right on St Tropez's central square.
Tahiti Beach, Le Pinet (tel: 94 97 18 02). Definitely a place for sand and sea.
Cheaper:
La Baronne Laetitia, rue Allard (tel: 94 97 04 02). Set in one of the narrow streets in town, more modest than smart.
Lou Cagnard, rue Paul-Roussel (tel: 94 97 04 24).

Nightlife
Start the latter part of the

evening at the bar of **La Marine** on the front – or at the **Hôtel Sube** at Bryan's Bar (first floor, on the front, reached through a passageway behind the statue of the Bailli de Suffren). Fashion changes fast in St Tropez but after this, for the ultra-smart league, it's still **Les Caves du Roy** in elegant **Hôtel Byblos.** The hotel itself is worth a visit, with hidden courtyards and surprising levels, art exhibitions and plenty of art as a feature of its own interior. Finish the night at **Le Bal,** somewhat gay in atmosphere, best from 4am till daylight. Alternatively **Papagayo,** on the harbour just behind the Annonciade Museum. Régine tried and failed with a Jimmy'z in this venue which has now reverted to its original name. John Morgan plays the piano in the bar downstairs and nearly brings the walls down.

Restaurants
Some top spots for eating out:
Chez Nano, place de l'Hôtel de Ville (tel: 94 97 01 66). Tables set out in the street, bordered by cypresses in pots. An agreeable venue tucked in behind the harbour and across from the pink town hall. Smart in style but welcoming to all.
La Marine, quai Jean Jaurès (tel: 94 97 04 07). Fashionable fish restaurant on the harbour. Yachtsman's decor.
Le Chabichou, ave Foch (tel: 94 54 80 00). An independent restaurant in the Hôtel Byblos. Expensive and exquisite, no place for those in a rush.
Leï Mouscardins, 16 rue Portalet (tel: 94 97 01 53). Set on the waterfront by the old tower at the end of the quai Frédéric. Top quality, top prices; not many young people.
There are cheaper restaurants available which still offer good quality meals:
Bar à vins, rue des Féniers (tel: 94 97 46 10). Wine bar with food

Atmosphere and setting are the essential elements in restaurants such as the popular Café des Arts

St Tropez treats style seriously, with high fashion at high prices

— and pool table. A favourite with yacht crews.
Bistrot de Pierre, place de la Garonne (tel: 94 97 22 49). Though on the edge of a small car park, pleasant enough for lunching outdoors.
Café des Arts, place des Lices (tel: 94 97 02 25). Choice from a limited but interesting menu. Can get very hot, but atmosphere is what counts.
La Flo, rue des Féniers (tel: 94 54 85 85). Just next to Le Canastel. American and English dishes for a young fun crowd.
Le Canastel, rue de la Citadelle (tel: 94 97 26 60). Brothers Jo-Jo and Guy know everybody and lay on a good pizza and *plat de jour*.
The best cafés/bars in St Tropez are:
Le Gorille, on the front. Steak Tartare, hamburgers, etc, as well as beer and coffee. Remains fashionable despite recent death of its proprietor —

the original Gorilla, friend to Picasso and the famous.
Sénéquier, on the front. A must for breakfast. One of the best known spots of St Tropez.

Shopping
St Tropez is well-known for the kind of avant-garde couture you pay a lot for and might not want to wear in many other places — although, of course, it might make you a huge success in Les Caves du Roy and other nightspots. Most of the top shops and boutiques are up in the old town, to be discovered as you stroll the narrow streets. One or two names to look out for are Jean Claude Jitrois, style in leather, with branches in the USA and Japan; Peau d'Ane, classy but not classical; Claude Bonucci; and Sonja Rykiel. There is also a lively trade in up-to-the-minute flea market fashion, particularly along the front.

Special Events
There are two festivals which go under the name of Les

ST TROPEZ AND THE SOUTHWEST COAST

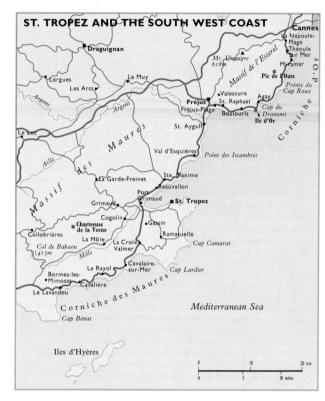

ST. TROPEZ AND THE SOUTH WEST COAST

Bravades, both full of costume and noisy, playful pageantry in a style entirely typical of St Tropez. The first is on 16 and 17 May, the second on 18 June. The May Bravade is a celebration of St Torpes. His effigy is removed from the church and paraded though the streets by town dignitaries in grand uniforms and armed with ancient blunderbusses. There is much shooting of blanks and plenty of liquid refreshment. The second Bravade, celebrating a victory over a Spanish fleet in 1637,

follows much the same formula as the first.

In September, in a nautical procession named the Nioulargo and referred to flatteringly as a race, yachts large and small sail round the headland to the beaches of Le Pampelonne. The procession is an occasion of great beauty. This is one of many yachting and sporting events laid on to make the season jollier still.

Over Christmas and the New Year, as happens now in most of the main resorts, there is a special programme of entertainments.

WHAT TO SEE ON THE SOUTHWEST COAST

◆
COGOLIN

A stone's throw across the untidy valley from spectacular Grimaud, Cogolin is often dismissed as unattractive by comparison. The impression can be adjusted by a stroll in the old town climbing up behind the Hôtel de Ville. Here there are vaulted passageways under buildings and a huddle of ancient houses in their tiny lanes. Cogolin is famous locally as an artisan centre and there is plenty of craft activity for visitors

to watch. Tobacco pipes are made from briar stumps at **Ch. Courrieu** at 58, ave Clémenceau. Prices seem unsurprising for routine pipes but a 'special', always made from a monster briar stump and often bearing fairly repulsive carvings, can fetch an astonishing sum. At **Tapis de Cogolin** boulevard Louis Blanc (off ave Clémenceau), sturdy women weave carpets by hand on mighty timber looms. The little town also turns out pottery, pewter and reeds for wind instruments. There is a little

Painters of the past and present have responded to the colour and light of St Tropez; and some carve their niche in the tourist trade

church which lately celebrated
its 900th anniversary and even a
Lebanese restaurant, Le
Bédouin, tucked behind the
church.

♦♦♦
CORNICHE D'OR

This is the name for the coast
road which twists round the
seaward side of the Esterel
Massif. Nothing on the Riviera is
more striking than the deep red
rock of the Massif as it plunges
into the blue abysses of the
Mediterranean. The rock
formations are splendid and
continuously surprising, the red
shining out through a partial
covering of green scrub.
Leaving St Raphael, the road
passes the deeply-settled villas
of **Boulouris** (there is nothing as
private or well-guarded as a
well-to-do French villa).
American troops came ashore
here during the landings of
August 1944. There is a tower
on a rock out to sea – the **Ile
d'Or,** whence the Corniche d'Or
has taken its otherwise
inappropriate name – and the
big bulk of **Cap Dramont** with a
signal station on top. Then the
road turns inland to round the
bay of **Agay,** a deep water
anchorage. None of the little
resorts here are of particular
importance or beauty, but the
mountain backdrop gives them
a special quality. Soon the most
impressive crag of all, the
strangely configured **Cap Roux**
with rocks like mighty
organ-pipes, becomes entirely
dominant. The water, now
bright blue, now cobalt, breaks
around fiery rocks. There are
tiny bays and fissures, lips and

ridges, iguana backs of rock
going down into the sea. The
scrub is full of herbs and
prickly, though here and there
interspersed with pine. In some
places, calamitously, the larger
trees have perished by forest
fire and stand about the place
like blackened, twisted
telephone poles.
After Cap Roux comes **Miramar,**
a pretty little place, and then the
delightfully curvaceous
coastline by **Théoule,** itself
under a great clump of rock
shaped like a baboon's skull.
Here the railway, which has
briefly turned inshore, rejoins
the coast road and the
spectacular journey round the
Corniche d'Or is accomplished.

♦♦
ESTEREL MASSIF

This striking group of low but
rugged mountains, mostly a
deep red porphyry with a
partial covering of scrub and
pine, is said to be of
exceedingly great age. It is
worn down now by the
elements but remains far more
mountainous in character than
might be suggested by the
altitude of its highest peak, **Mont
Vinaigre,** only 2,000ft (618m)
high. The Esterel massif was for
centuries a haunt of brigands
and a refuge for escaped
galley-slaves from Toulon. For
travellers, a safe crossing was a
source of relief and satisfaction.
Today the Corniche d'Or coast
road flanks it to the east. The
twisting N7 crosses the top of
the massif diagonally from
Fréjus to Cannes, offering
splendid views both north and
south and passing close to **Mt**

The remains of a once-thriving Roman city still stand in Fréjus, established by Julius Caesar and named Forum Julii in his honour

Vinaigre. A 15-minute walk (follow the signpost) will take the active to the summit. A marvellous little road also climbs up from **Cap Roux** on the coast (requiring great attention from drivers). At the top of the climb there is a right turn to the **Pic de l'Ours,** another of the high points of the massif, somewhat disfigured by a TV mast. The left turn takes you back down again to Agay with the possibility here of turning right again up into the hills to enter St Raphael by the wooded groves of Valescure.
The Esterel Massif forms a knobbly skyline as you look south from Cannes and it occupies a fair chunk of the view northwards along much of the coast from Fréjus down. Its characteristic lumpy ridges and extravagant rock formations make it deeply loved. In the right weather its colours are magnificent. Unfortunately, a series of forest fires in 1986, most probably set by arsonists, swept from the N7 to the sea, destroying most of the pines. But the general impression is still one of green, like an animal's thick pelt against a deep red skin.

◆◆
FRÉJUS
One of the most interesting spots on the Riviera, Fréjus sits on a small hill a mile (1.6km) or so from the sea and gives the impression of being a thoroughgoing Provençal town – something of an illusion as a glance at its dense history makes clear.
Native tribes and ancient Greeks appear to have frequented the site, but it was Julius Caesar who first gave it definitive form, establishing it as a staging post on the Aurelian Way, the Roman road from Italy.

ST TROPEZ AND THE SOUTHWEST COAST

From Caesar, it acquired the name Forum Julii, now transmuted into Fréjus. Next it became a major naval base for the still-expanding Roman empire. Swift galleys based in Forum Julii defeated the heavier warships of Antony and Cleopatra at the battle of Actium in 31BC. Augustus, victor of Actium, settled many of his veterans in Forum Julii as colonists. At the height of its Roman period, the city had a population of 40,000 and possessed not merely a port but also an amphitheatre, a theatre, public baths and all the rest of it. Water came on a 25 mile (40km) long aqueduct. Parts of the aqueduct, the amphitheatre and many other Roman remains can still be seen today.

After the Romans, Fréjus became a major reception point for Christian converts, accepting them into the church in a handsome octagonal baptistry which still stands in the centre of the town. It was constructed in the late 4th/early 5th century and is one of the most venerable Christian buildings in France. Matters were quiet now till the Saracens destroyed the town early in the 10th century. One Bishop Riculphe built it up again. Fréjus acquired fresh ramparts and a fortified

For all the fame and fortune which it has earned over the past century, St Tropez has retained the charm of a small harbour town

cathedral complex at its centre, attached to the old baptistry. This group of buildings still remains the central kernel of the town.

For some centuries after this Fréjus shared in the common history of Provence. But for the past 200 years or so it has also been a base-camp for French troops recruited overseas, hence the Buddhist and Muslim temples in the area. Following Algerian independence, many French Algerians were resettled here. In 1959 Fréjus was the site of a major disaster when a dam wall ruptured above the town. Hundreds were drowned.

Today, despite the town's long and varied history, the little market square by the cathedral and the streets radiating out from it do indeed feel properly Provençal. With many camp-sites round about, both Fréjus and Fréjus Plage, its near neighbour, are crowded and somewhat downmarket in summer. Winter would be an excellent time to visit the many monuments.

The remains of Forum Julii in Roman Fréjus are a major point of interest. **Les Arènes,** the Roman amphitheatre, is at the western edge of town. Its somewhat ruinous exterior makes it look as if it has been washed over by the sea for many centuries. Within, there is some modern stone seating, some wooden tiers to provide viewing space for modern entertainments – rock concerts, dog shows, tennis and bullfights. The Roman spirit evidently persists.

The **Roman Theatre** is in delicate condition and is now used mainly for concerts. Guided tours only are allowed. **The port** covered 54 acres and had a mile (1.6km) of quays. It was sited on what is now flat ground, some way inland, at the foot of the hill on which the town stands. The port was filled in at the time of the French Revolution, but because the infill was of poor quality the land has never been built on – cabbages and carrots cover it today. Substantial Roman remnants can still be seen. **St Anthony's Mound,** one need hardly say, is a mound topped with ivy-coloured Roman ruins. The **Lantern of Augustus** is an elegant medieval tower, hexagonal, and built on a Roman base. Fréjus is now involved in a major undertaking concerning the Roman port. The first stage will be the construction of a modern marina just behind the present line of the beach. In due course this will be linked by canal to the old Roman port, which will be re-excavated and reconstructed.

The legs of the **Aqueduct** arches, all that remains in the immediate vicinity of the town, go striding away across the road that links Fréjus to the N7. Note the modern primary school built in Roman style adjacent to the aqueduct. Further from town, substantial stretches of the aqueduct survive.

There are also town gates and other Roman bits and pieces to be discovered as one strolls about.

The cathedral, its dumpy red tower capped by a spire with green and yellow tiles, is the focal point of town. The main entrance is from a square which also houses the town hall. Roman remains and a medieval cemetery were discovered in this square in 1988 and swiftly covered up again. The doors of the cathedral (walnut, 1530) are remarkable for 16 elaborate carvings (scenes from the life of Christ, portraits of Provençal rulers, etc) which the cathedral guide will explain extremely fully, in French only. A headless child and crossed scimitars in a side panel of the door provide a reminder of Saracen days. Inside, immediately to the left, is the entrance to the baptistry. This has interesting niches; Roman columns and capitals are incorporated and there are various fonts and lustral basins. To the right on entry is the small cathedral, with, on its left hand side, a small and serious-minded 10th/11th-century nave. This opens, through sweeping 13th-century arches, into a high rib-vaulted nave of the later period.

Passing between cathedral and baptistry, the visitor now climbs a few steps to the small cloister, a delectable spot. Pointed arches are supported on twin marble columns, and oleanders grow in the centre around an extremely ancient well. A few tiny painted panels in the cloister ceiling survive from the 15th century. In the upper storey, rebuilt on just one side, is the town's **Archaeological Museum.** The centrepiece is an elaborate but rather dull Roman mosaic floor. There are fine Greek vases (brought by the

Destroyed on the orders of Louis XIII, the fortress at Grimaud, named after the Grimaldi family, is now reduced to a romantic ruin

Romans) and a bust of a double-visaged Hermes – brilliant but only a replica. The original has been lost to Paris. A mile (1.6km) north of the town, just off the N7, is a **Buddhist shrine and pagoda,** built by French Indochinese troops in 1919. The gently reclining Buddha and other statuary are set amid pines, in a garden with a pagoda.

◆
FRÉJUS PLAGE
Sandy beaches, extremely popular and crowded, are backed by a promenade with craftsmen's stalls and, on the far side of the road, a multitude of restaurants and cafés. A linear resort, running into St Raphael, along the coastal strip of Fréjus.

♦♦
GRIMAUD

If ever a ruin stood romantically on a peak, it is the 11th-century **fortress** at Grimaud, a town which takes its name from the Grimaldi family. You see it from St Tropez against the background of the Maures massif; from nearby Cogolin you see it against the sky, the essence of military might now changed into an object of aesthetic pleasure. Beneath the castle, old streets with arches and doorways framed in green serpentine stone — one of the features of the area — lead towards a Romanesque **church,** 11th century, like the castle. The church is deeply sculptural in form, with barrel vault and rounded apse and wide semi-circular arches. A coin deposited in an *éclairage* machine to the left on entry will throw a sentimental spotlight on

statuary. Then the light broadens to offer a cinematic illumination of the whole. Grimaud is lovely; but one of those hill towns and villages made so neat and tidy for visitors that it is less of a place, more of a monument.

♦
MASSIF DES MAURES

Circular route from St Tropez
The Maures mountains, shaggily wooded with cork-oak and chestnuts, lie to the west and north of the St Tropez gulf. The massif is a series of jumbled waves of mountain, not very huge to look at from outside but offering, particularly from several ridge roads, a real sensation of height. The towns and villages in the massif have often come under attack and substantial areas were held for centuries by the Saracens.
A very long day's tour could begin by striking south across the St Tropez peninsula, through a valley of vines, to the little health resort of **la Croix Valmer,** up on a shoulder of hill. The village is nothing special, though the wine and the sea views down to the south are good. The road now winds down to Cavalaire-sur-Mer on the southern side of the Maures massif. This is another undistinguished town, though spaciously set out on a broad triangular plain. Now the road becomes quite beautiful, crossing a cape to emerge, at a fair height, above a gloriously wild and rocky coast with views south to the long and sinuous backbones of the **Iles d'Hyères.** A side road winds down among

terraces planted with a rich variety of trees, to the sandy cove of **Le Rayol** (its beauties somewhat diminished by the presence of one good but over-large hotel). Soon after this, passing through Canadel and Pramousquier, the forest thins and the hills turn to gaunter rock and scrub.

Le Lavandou is a proper little town, with marina and, alas, some outsize buildings on its front. Soon afterwards, leave the Toulon road, taking the N98 in the direction of **La Mole.** The La Mole road winds eastward to Cogolin through a wooded valley with some vines. This would lead one back to St Tropez, making a shorter but agreeable tour. A second possibility is to take the fine ridge road to the right, 2 miles (3km) before the main Cogolin turning, in order to come out eventually at the same point and so complete the shorter tour a little more adventurously. Better still, hold left instead for **Collobrières.** Now one climbs on a tiny road through many S-bends and dense woods to reach the **Col de Babaou,** 1,350ft (414m) high and offering fine views down — on one side towards Hyères and, almost simultaneously, over the northern edge of the massif. A road to the right here leads down into the valley of Collobrières, suddenly broader and full of vines producing rosé wines. Collobrières is a small place with stream and bridges, the tiniest town square and many plane trees. In addition to wine, the main local products are honey and anything made

from chestnuts.

On exit, take the Grimaud road and after 4 miles (6km) a side turn to **La Chartreuse de la Verne,** a well-signposted but mostly rough dirt surface with crags and craters worthy of respect. After another 4 miles (6km) along the northern side of a valley, the shaken traveller reaches a spur of hill stretching out across the way — and on it, the splendid **Charterhouse of la Verne.** This elaborate establishment, set in utter solitude among mountains and forest, was built in the 12th century and later reconstructed several times. Ruined at the time of the French Revolution, it has been under reconstruction again since 1982 by members of the Order of St Bruno. The site is beautiful, the buildings most evocative, the brown and muddy-looking walls pierced by gateways and doors ringed in serpentine stone. The visitors' book in the chapel is witness to the deep emotions stirred among those who come here. After returning to the asphalt road, it is possible to turn right and so return to St Tropez by way of Grimaud 12 ½ miles (20km) distant, once again shortening the tour. Even better, however, is to travel a little further back towards Collobrières, then turn right to take a winding road up on to the northern ridge of the massif and back by way of **La Garde Freinet.** The several miles of ridge are narrow and exhilarating. La Garde Freinet, seen from above before entry, is a tight huddle of Provençal roofs. On arrival it is revealed as

a pretty little town with
lozenge-shaped squares and
narrow streets. The Saracens
used it as a stronghold during
their period of domination.
The route now leads back to St
Tropez via Grimaud and
Cogolin; but even this tour
leaves considerable areas of the
Maures massif still to be
explored.

◆
PORT GRIMAUD
Many settlements, like Grimaud
itself, were high on hills in
strong defensive positions. But
frequently they required access
to the sea for fishing and the
transport of goods and people.
Small ports were set up on the
shoreline as dependencies of

the main settlement. This was
the case with Grimaud but the
early harbour-settlement has
now given place to an
extraordinary architectural
fantasy — a purpose-built,
designer town that looks as if it
might have been there for
centuries except that each of its
varied and engaging houses has
its own yacht-mooring in a
complex pattern of lagoons and
canals. Locals and holidaymakers describe Port Grimaud
as a modern Venice, but the
comparison is not a good one.
There is a higher proportion of
water and no decay at all. All

*Port Grimaud, a modern port built to
look like an authentic Mediterranean
fishing village*

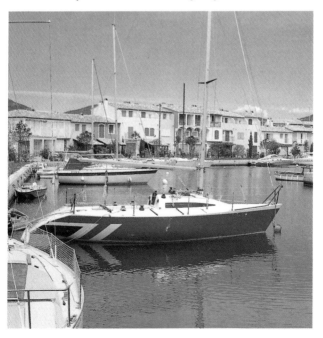

town-planners should pay it a compulsory visit as part of their training.

◆
STE MAXIME
This growing resort behind a hoop of mainly sandy beach looks south across the gulf to St Tropez. Most of the buildings on the front are newish but there is one short row of older shops — tobacconist, café, etc — set back a little with pollarded plane trees to make a kind of public space. Behind, there are pleasant 19th-century streets and an older, miniscule market place. Just to the east along the front is the only real monument, the medieval **Tour Carrée** or Square Tower, recently opened as a pleasing local museum (closed Tuesdays). In the short **rue Gabriel Péri** just behind there is a little shop stuffed with glassware and ceramics from Biot. The resort has a family atmosphere and a cream-coloured bailey bridge on exit. Otherwise, there is little to distinguish it from other lesser resorts.

◆
ST RAPHAEL
St Raphael was for centuries a tiny coastal settlement. Its fishing community lived round a fortress-church a short way back from the sea and crowded into it in times of danger. It became a resort thanks to the enthusiasm of one Alphonse Karr, a former editor of *Figaro*, who settled here and enthused about it to his talented circle. The composer Gounod was one who joined him and here wrote his *Roméo et Juliette* (1866).

Berlioz, Maupassant and Dumas also visited. Nearly three-quarters of a century earlier, in 1799, Napoleon had arrived in triumph from Egypt. It was from here, also, that he set sail for exile in Elba, a prisoner on an English frigate. Nowadays, big modern buildings line a front which proceeds through a right angle and several bends, giving it and its harbours an interesting configuration. Behind, the pastel-coloured 19th century buildings, though exceedingly busy in summer, look physically much like any French provincial town of the period. A visit should take in the **Romanesque church,** extremely serious and gaunt and with a castle-like

St Raphael owes its currently fashionable status to the praises of journalist Alphonse Karr

tower. It stands just by the lively fishmarket of the place de la République with old, small streets all round. There is one very interesting group of buildings in the centre, on and just behind the front. It includes the salmon-pink **casino,** a huge late **19th-century church,** Byzantine style, and a former hotel with plaster scallops and balconies — its name, most fittingly for its period, was the **Winter Palace.** The old hotel is now divided into apartments full of physiotherapists. In this little group lies much of the history of the Riviera; and it seems peculiarly fitting that both church and casino are floodlit at night.

Just behind St Raphael is **Valescure,** with delightful pinewoods, golf courses and good hotels. The settlement began as a health resort for veterans of the Roman legions and is still today a very pleasant place to stay.

◆◆
ST TROPEZ PENINSULA

St Tropez lies on the northern shores of a peninsula which is beautiful in its own right, with beaches (see St Tropez above), vines and hills. There are also a number of villages well worth a visit.

Driving southward past the long beach of **le Pampelonne,** with its many hedonistic little private sections, the road climbs steeply up to **Ramatuelle,** situated on a hillside which feels disproportionately lofty as you look down. The village is supported on buttresses as if the whole of it might slip down the hill like a single bird's nest. The inner parts are extraordinarily compressed, with tiny circuitous alleyways and secret-looking doors and masses of plants on window ledges and in pots and barrels. There are serpentine stone doorways and the regulation Romanesque church. There is a Tahitian restaurant worthy of a visit and a pizzeria — Il Vesuvio — which is not. The uphill continuation of the road now leads to a series of ruined towers, former windmills known as **Les Moulins de Paillas.** They are set on a high ridge with lofty views, southwards in the direction of **le Lavandou** (see **Massif des Maures** above) and back towards the beaches of le Pampelonne. A tiny road leading a short way along the spur offers high views over the Gulf of St Tropez to the north.

Colourful cafés and restaurants are a lively feature of the towns and resorts along the southwest coast of the French Riviera

Down a little from the windmills but still high, the village of **Gassin** rides a ridge of its own, long and thin as a warship. The church tower here is the highest point of all, but along the highest piece of actual ground there is a terrace of restaurants, all in a fine situation. A walk around this beautiful hill village discloses wide views in all directions. Ramatuelle is outstanding; Gassin is superb – though both, like Grimaud, are excessively prettified, almost sanitised, with never a dab of mortar out of place.

Accommodation

Fréjus:

Hôtel les Résidences du Colombier, Route de Bagnols, nearly 2 miles (3km) from town (tel: 94 51 45 92). Comfortable rooms are set in single storey rows in gardens, lots of space. Nearby at St Aygulf, just west of Fréjus, **Hotel Plein Soleil** (tel: 94 81 09 57). Small and well-furnished, takes pride in its breakfasts.

St Raphael district:

Golf de Valescure (tel: 94 52 01 57). Ideal for committed golfers, easy access to course, pleasant pinewood setting for this modern hotel.

Restaurants

Fréjus has a number of interesting restaurants. **Lou Calen,** 9 rue Desaugiers (tel: 94 52 36 87), just by the town hall, is delicious, with a Provençal accent; the menu changes to suit the season. **Tête d'Ail,** on the south side of market square, is more rough and ready, in a vaulted cellar with a 13th-century bread oven in the toilet. **Hôtel les Résidences du Colombier,** (tel: 94 51 45 92) is a short way out of town on the Route de Bagnols, and has made a promising start under new (Scottish) ownership. Fréjus is on the edge of the Côtes de Provence wine area, the first wine growing district one reaches travelling west from Nice and Cannes. The **Domaine des Plans,** above Fréjus on Roquebrune-sur-Argens Road, offers a good degustation with explanations of wine husbandry as well as wine manufacture.

THE CANNES COAST

This brief central stretch of the Riviera reaches from La Napoule on the northern edge of the Esterel massif along through Cannes and Antibes to Cros-de-Cagnes. The first part offers fine views south towards the Esterel. From sea-level Cannes, one looks out over two little inshore islands called the Iles des Lérins, and, from high points around the town, back towards the Alps. The Cap d'Antibes, protruding southwards from Antibes, is famous as a haunt of the rich and talented, and is one of several similar promontories on the Riviera. All this is a delight for the visitor; it is very interesting and much of it very beautiful; and the same may be said of both Cannes and Antibes.

The final part of the coast is the dullest on the Riviera, flat and unappealing. The *arrière-pays*, on the other hand, is specially rich in ancient and delightful towns. These include Grasse, the perfume capital of France, Vence and St-Paul-de-Vence and others which are just as attractive, though perhaps a little less known.

CANNES

A single glance from the right spot reveals the layout of Cannes, arguably the most famous and most glamorous of all Riviera towns. That spot is the walled enclosure of church and castle crowning the rocky outcrop of **Le Suquet,** the Old Town. Start at the Old Harbour beneath and take the pretty little rue St Antoine behind it, full of tiny restaurants and geraniums. Then, almost immediately, turn up the steep

Although the name Cannes now conjures up images of wealth and glamour, the Old Harbour has not lost its character and beauty

THE CANNES COAST

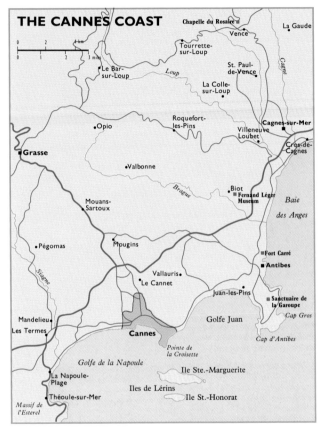

THE CANNES COAST

steps of the rue de la Boucherie, and you will soon come — though rather breathlessly — to the summit. From here, looking down past the roofs of the medieval dwellings at your feet, it is possible to see the configuration of the town as clearly as in a diagram. First comes your original starting place, the Old Harbour or **Vieux Port,** crammed to bursting with delicious yachts.

Beyond the Old Harbour, sweeping away to the west to end in another marina and a distant white casino, lies a curving bay backed by palms and pines.

Shining through from behind the trees is a high white wall of apartments and hotels. Among these are the Majestic, the Martinez and the Carlton, each one in its solid luxury and period splendour an embodiment of what the word 'Riviera' originally meant. The gently curving hoop of trees and buildings, with its fringe of extremely smart and expensive shops at ground floor level, bears the name **La Croisette;** it ranks in the Riviera Hall of Fame with the Promenade des Anglais at Nice.

Between the Old Harbour and the boulevard de la Croisette, however, there stands a massive modern building which may be of equal interest. The pink concrete **Palais des Festivals** provides a home for the annual Cannes Film Festival and all the other festivals and conferences to which Cannes now acts as an almost over-eager host. Conferences range from worthy meetings on the subject of golf course construction to the International Festival of Games, featuring Scrabble, chess and bridge. Though these may be of doubtful status as major international happenings, the Film Festival, at least, still reigns supreme. In addition to showing some of the most inter-esting films of our time, it pulls in its quota of glamorous stars and prominent directors. These in their turn attract hosts of visi-tors, hoping a little of the magic will rub off on them. Outside the Palais des Festivals there is a chunk of pavement bearing the palmprints — to take names at random — of Jeanne Moreau and Charlotte Rampling, Micky Mouse and Franco Zeffirelli, Roman Polanski and Catherine Deneuve.

The town behind the front is really not so big. There are a number of shopping streets of great interest (see below). Cannes' claim to elegance lies as much in its shops as in its hotels. Behind these shopping streets the town is sharply divided by the railway line and station, with a large road running along on top of them. There are extremely attractive, pastel-shaded, 19th-century streets beyond this highway, but almost everything with which the visitor will be concerned lies between it and the sandy beach of La Croisette. The only major exception is the

The distinctive Carlton hotel, on the long, palm-fringed boulevard of La Croisette, where residents regularly take their promenade

THE CANNES COAST

Observatory on the high hill above the bay in the district of Super-Cannes (see **What to see,** below).

Winter Visitors

Cannes got its start as a Riviera town from an English ex-chancellor, Lord Brougham. In 1834, on his way into Savoy with his ailing daughter, Brougham found the Nice frontier closed to prevent the spread of a cholera outbreak from France. Retreating west along the coast, he 'discovered' a quaint and delightful little fishing village of 4,000 souls, taking its name from the canes or *cannes* which grew in the marshes round about. Here he built a house, though his daughter did not live to see it finished, and here he wintered for the following 34 years. It was not long before a swarm of British aristocrats had followed him; and to these were added the grand and wealthy of other nations. Titles and coronets and crowns abounded in the former fishing village and little by little the grand hotels were built to serve this kind of customer. In the 1890s one resident counted 60 'royals' from many nations. Edward, Prince of Wales, came every year up to Victoria's death in 1901. He indulged in various amatory frolics and on one occasion was in such great haste to reach the theatre that he left the bottom button of his waistcoat undone. He was copied instantly, setting a fashion which has lasted to this day.

French writers frequented Cannes, among them Prosper

The long sweep of La Croisette beach offers views of La Napoule Bay and of the sea-front crowds

Merimée and Guy de Maupassant. The painter Pierre Bonnard was also a visitor. So was the American dancer Isadora Duncan some years later; it was here that she met her death, strangled when her long scarf became entangled round the axle of her open car. At some point the city developed an American accent. La Californie is just one of many North American place names in Cannes and the town is twinned, most fittingly, with Beverly Hills. Cannes has celebrated American Independence Day for 50 years.

Sandy beaches are one of

Cannes' major attractions. The beach to the west of Le Suquet stretches out a good distance towards La Napoule, while in summer the big hotels backing La Croisette have fenced-off reservations along much of the foreshore, brilliant with umbrellas differing in colour and design in each establishment. But really, what matters most today as in grander times, is strolling along the pavement above the beach, backwards and forwards the length of La Croisette, the purpose and pleasure to see and to be seen. Enjoying the shops ranks almost equal and Cannes also has some stunning restaurants — not all of them expensive.

Like the other major Riviera towns, Cannes began as a wintering place and then became a summer resort. Even so, it has always held on to some part of its winter clientele; and today's year-round diet of festivals and conferences means there is scarcely a moment when the town is less than busy. The visitor has to concede that there is some truth in the bathetic tourist slogan 'Cannes: The Best Time To Be There Is Anytime'. This world-famous resort lacks the big city feel of Nice — some would think this an advantage — but it offers a beautiful setting and a good deal of elegance through the whole of the calendar.

Historic Characters

The origins and early history of Cannes are deeply involved with the Iles des Lérins, the small, flat little islands that lie just off the coast, visible from almost everywhere. The smaller of the two bears the name of St Honorat, who founded a monastery here at the end of the 4th century. His sister Ste Marguerite founded a nunnery on the larger island, likewise named after her. There is a story that St Honorat agreed to see his sister only when a particular almond tree was in flower — that is to say, once a year. She prayed so hard that it flowered monthly.

The islands made up a great religious centre and sent out many saints. St Patrick spent nine years here before beginning his holy task in Ireland. The monks also had suzerainty over the nearby mainland and it was they who were responsible for erecting the defences of Le Suquet. Cannes ceased to be a religious fief only in 1788 when the monastery was closed. It was reopened in 1869 as a Cistercian establishment. There was, though, a state prison on Ste Marguerite. It was here that the Man in the Iron Mask was imprisoned from 1687 to 1698. His identity has never been resolved. Also imprisoned here by Louis XIV were six Huguenot pastors. They were kept in solitary confinement for periods of up to 30 years and all but one went mad. Another prisoner was Marshal Bazaine, accused of betraying the

Emperor Napoleon III in 1870. He, however, managed to escape.

WHAT TO SEE

◆◆
ILES DES LÉRINS (THE LÉRINS ISLANDS)
On St Honorat, the honey-coloured keep of the old **monastery** is a romantic building offering fine views. The 19th-century monastery is adjacent. The monks produce lavender, oranges, honey and a sweet liqueur, Lerina. On Ste Marguerite, visitors to the 17th-century **fort** of the same name are shown, among other gruesome relics, the cell once occupied by the Man in the Iron Mask. The fort itself is now a youth centre.

St Honorat Island, named after the 4th-century saint, is wooded with pines and eucalyptus trees

Both islands are well wooded and agreeable for a gentle walk, a picnic or a swim off the rocks.

Frequent departures by boat to St Honorat (journey time 30 mins) and Ste Marguerite (15 mins): boats depart from Gare Maritime, just beside Palais des Festivals on the Old Port side (tel: 93 39 11 82 for details).

◆
LA CASTRE MUSEUM
in Cannes' former castle in Le Suquet.

African, American Indian and Oceanic ethnographic material along with modern sculpture and 19th-century paintings. One or two of these show Cannes as it was then. Stock's *Le Suquet at Sunset* (1864), for instance, reveals an utterly untouched hilltop town with church and fortress. Buttura Ernest's view of La Croisette in 1876, by contrast, shows carriages, top hats and parasols against a view of the Old Town across the water.
Closed: Mondays and 1 November to 15 December.

◆
OBSERVATORY
Super-Cannes.

The well-signposted approach road (leave town by ave Isola-Bella) winds up and up among apartments and villas, offering a spacious version of the city and its private gardens. The road returns finally to a point surprisingly near the coast and here the observatory platform (reached by lift) offers splendid views up into the Alps and down over Cannes and the Lérins islands.

Open: all year, morning till nightfall.

Accommodation
Cannes is a hotel town. It has a goodly number of the Riviera's historic hotels and these are still fine places to stay if grandeur is your line. There is a wide selection of less expensive places and some where prices are relatively modest.

Expensive (and grand):
Carlton, 58 la Croisette (tel: 93 68 91 68). Memories of earlier, aristocratic days in one of the great sea-front hotels, built 1912. Luxury unabated.
Majestic, 6 la Croisette (tel: 93 68 91 00). Built 1926. Very comfortable though reputation less glitzy than the Carlton's.
Martinez, 73 la Croisette (tel: 93 68 91 91). Another of the grand ones, currently enjoying a renaissance.
Montfleury, 25 ave Beauséjour, very different from hotels above – modern style, set in 10-acre park.

Reasonable:
Beau Séjour, 5 rue des Fauvettes (tel: 93 39 63 00).
Embassy, 6 rue de Bône (tel: 93 38 79 02).

Cheaper:
Roches Fleuries, 92 rue George-Clémenceau. An unpretentious hotel in west Cannes.
Hotel Amiraute, small, central, simple.

Nightlife
Le Studio Circus, 48 bd de la République (tel: 93 38 32 98) has been fashionable lately among the young with slides and a light show to accompany the disco

THE CANNES COAST

music. **Whisky à Gogo,** 115 ave des Lérins (tel: 93 43 20 63) is still alive and well, while Jane's piano bar in the **Gray d'Albion,** 38 rue des Serbes (tel: 93 68 54 54) may help to soothe the older spirit.

Cannes also has three casinos, the **Municipal Casino** in the Palais des Festivals, the **Palm Beach** on the eastern tip of La Croisette and the **Casino des Fleurs,** 5 rue des Belges.

Restaurants

Naturally Cannes has smart and expensive places to eat, but there are everyday establishments as well, chief among them a row of fish restaurants behind the old harbour. In the lower part of Le Suquet, there are many appetising and attractive little places.

Popular with the 'smart set' are: **La Palme d'Or,** the restaurant of the Hotel Martinez, 73 boulevard de la Croisette (tel: 93 84 10 24). Large and swagger but with subtle and delicious food.

Closed: 20 November to 20 January.

Le Royal Gray, in Gray d'Albion complex, 38 rue des Serbes (tel: 93 68 54 54). Another gastronomic venue.

Fish and fun are available at: **Le Caveau Provençal,** 45 rue Félix Faure (tel: 93 39 06 33). Serves *bouillabaisse, bourride* and *fruits de mer,* with tables and a shell fish stall set out in front of the ground floor restaurant and more seating up on the first floor. Lively atmosphere.

Others in the same row of restaurants, looking on to the Old Port from the far side of a little park, are similar in style. **La Mère Besson,** 13 rue des Frères Pradignac (tel: 93 39 59 24) serves traditional Provençal food.

On the edge of Le Suquet, try almost any of the little restaurants in the rue St Antoine. **La Mirabelle,** at no. 24 (tel: 93 38 72 75), has a pretty balcony with geraniums outside; inside there are dishes on dressers and dried flowers. It is a serious eating place – not cheap. **La Papillote,** a little lower down the hill, is tiny and candle-lit.

For cafés and bars, La Croisette is the most obvious place, and here the **Café de Festival** sets the tone, offering directors' chairs with famous cinematic names on them. The bars of the great hotels may offer glimpses of the stars in person. There are more down-to-earth cafés behind the Old Harbour, with a pleasant atmosphere of *pastis* and newspaper-reading.

Shopping

Cannes offers the shopper every imaginable opportunity, from the necessities of daily life to the smartest clothes and the most exclusive jewellery. Many reckon Cannes, along with Monte-Carlo, second only to Paris in the French shopping galaxy. It is very complete and extraordinarily compact; in a walk of just half an hour or so – highly recommended even for the non-shopper – one can get a good idea of the whole range of goods and the main shopping places.

A handy starting point, because

Traditional fish dishes and a friendly atmosphere are the specialities at Le Caveau Provençal restaurant in Cannes

it is the most Provençal and most traditional, might be the covered food market just off the rue Louis Blanc, which runs up from the old harbour. It is bright and active and full of good things. The salads look appetising in the best Provençal manner: there are roses and gladioli and goat's cheeses and fresh fish (which tends to get sold out a little early).

From here, it is a step down to the rue Meynadier, which runs parallel to the sea three blocks back from it. The lower end, by Le Suquet, is Neapolitan-narrow, with little restaurants and pizzerias. Then it becomes everybody's shopping street, evidence that Cannes has things to do in its own right without benefit, necessarily, of tourists. There

are food shops of all kinds, *charcuteries* and butchers and delicious cheese shops, most odoriferous, and run-of-the-mill clothes shops, with jeans and shoes and clothes for teenagers, all very busy.

A right turn from Meynadier takes one to the rue d'Antibes, and closer to elegance. In the appearance of its buildings, this is any street from a well-to-do French provincial town, made up of old houses with apartments above shops, the façades an agreeable display of shutters and wrought iron. The shops themselves are a mixture, from standard high-street chains like Etam to some of the best names in clothes design. Chanel, Ungaro, Yves St Laurent, Emanuelle Kahn all have establishments in the rue d'Antibes. There is a smart homeopathic store and elegant displays of locally made candied fruit, a sudden great whiff of cheese from the Crèmerie Anglaise, antique shops and glass and porcelain shops and the Galerie de Cannes, selling modern art. The rue d'Antibes provides evidence that the French take children's fashion very seriously. La Diablerie (up to 12 years) sells well-designed leather jackets, beautifully cut trousers, and original shoes. Les Petits Durs — The Little Toughies — has casual clothes for children from three months to 16 years old. Jacadi has the classic French look for children. Turning right again from the rue

Pablo Picasso worked for a time in the castle in Antibes, which now houses a permanent exhibition of the work he produced there

d'Antibes, the shopper will enter a two-storey shopping mall — Les Boutiques de Gray Street, part of the Gray d'Albion hotel complex. This runs the whole way between the rue d'Antibes and La Croisette. There is a fountain, and long threads of water among greenery. The shops here, though much vaunted, may perhaps seem a little stodgy after those in the rue d'Antibes; and certainly they are expensive. There are real estate offices among boutiques selling fabrics, jewellery and smart bags. For traditional Provençal print fabrics, all very pretty, try Souleiado, a company with literally hundreds of outlets round the world.

Now the walk has brought us out into the open air of La Croisette. Here, among the great hotels, are all the great classical names and high-style shops. Hermes, Gucci, Cartier, Chanel again, Van Cleef & Arpels with a restrained and altogether beautiful display. For clothes, the standards are set by shops like Lanvin and Karl Lagerfeld – actually displaying its prices – and maintained by all the others. A real treat for those who enjoy this kind of style.

Special Events

January: MIDEM (International Market for Records and Music Publishing).
May: International Film Festival.
July/August: Great numbers of artistic events and all kinds of entertainments. Fireworks shows, *son et lumière* on Lérins Islands, etc.
October: FIPA (International Festival of Audio-visual Programmes) and MIPCOM (International Market for Video-communication).
December: 'Expo Cannes'.

WHAT TO SEE ON THE CANNES COAST

♦♦♦
ANTIBES

Antibes is a special place, with an atmosphere all of its own. A strong fort dominates the eastern end of town; there are ramparts with fine sea views; and tucked away behind them, in a fascinating mix of ancient and modern, a sturdy little castle and museum full of many of the most exuberant of all the works of Pablo Picasso. Behind these come narrow, winding

streets, leading towards the traffic-laden, newer parts of town. The total effect of the old town is one of small-scale cragginess, in genial intimacy with the sea.

Founded by the Greeks, Antibes was originally Antinopolis, 'the city opposite' – opposite Nice, that is to say, the Greek foundation on the far side of the Baie des Anges. Later, the towns became true opposites and enemies. Nice was the frontier town of Savoy, Antibes the frontier town of France. Hence the massive **Fort Carré** on the eastern edge of old Antibes, constructed mainly during the 16th century and finished in the 17th under Vauban. This is the main monument that you see as you drive through on the coastal highway. Napoleon was here in 1794, a young revolutionary general impoverished through the tardy arrival of his pay-cheques; he was briefly imprisoned in the Fort Carré on the fall of Robespierre.

A Walk round Antibes

A good walk could begin near the fort, on the ramparts bounding the old harbour to the west. Following the front westwards on the Promenade Amiral-de-Grasse, there are good views back towards Nice and the mountains, out to sea to the south and on towards the Cap d'Antibes. In a short while you pass the back of the cathedral and castle terrace and then, after a rather longer stretch, arrive at the **Archaeological Museum** in the St André Bastion. The exhibits

THE CANNES COAST

reach back to Etruscan, Greek and Roman times; many of the most interesting have been recovered from the sea.

Now the walker might double back towards the port, turning in between the cathedral and the castle and passing both to reach the elongated little market square beyond. This is the **Cours Masséna,** scene of a charmingly busy morning market and an excellent place to refresh oneself in a café or market restaurant before the major undertaking of Antibes. This is a visit to the cathedral and castle.

The **cathedral** is in fact a church, though still fondly known by a title which it relinquished centuries ago. Parts of it are ancient. A Romanesque tower stands just by the main façade which is itself 17th century and in slightly ruinous condition. Inside, there are various works of religious art including, in the south transept, an altarpiece by Louis Bréa (c 1515). He was one of the so-called 'Nice school', a phrase referring to a group of painters standing at the meeting point between the Middle Ages and subsequent developments arriving from Italy. Some fine examples of this work are still to be seen in churches, cathedrals and museums on the Riviera (there is also a contemporary Nice School).

Re-emerging from the cathedral and mounting a small ramp past cannons and cannon balls, one comes to the **castle** entrance. Castle and cathedral seem to form a pair and the castle, too, has a Romanesque tower. Most

of the rest of it is 16th century. It was a stronghold of the Grimaldi family (see **Monaco,** below). By World War II it had become a museum and here, in 1946, the museum director gave space to Picasso for use as a studio. Picasso had come to stay in nearby Golfe Juan after the war years in Paris, but he had nowhere suitable to work. Now, in the old Grimaldi Castle in Antibes, with the melancholy of war behind him, he let the Mediterranean side of his fantasy find full expression. Masterpiece followed masterpiece, whether it was a painting of a goat, or a scene with a fish, or Ulysses with siren, or a centaur with a grin and trident. Picasso worked here for just six months, from July to December, in one of the great creative episodes of the century — then left the whole of his work of the period behind him on permanent loan to the museum. The paintings are now accompanied by a wonderful collection of Picasso's ceramics from a little later in his life (see **Vallauris,** below). There are photographs and drawings, lithographs and sculptures. This is a museum where many who think themselves indifferent to Picasso discover the astonishing verve and geniality of some of his best work.

The visit begins with a mixture of paintings by other artists on the ground floor, some outstanding. The castle terrace has a set of striking sculptures by Germaine Richier. The bulk of the Picasso material is up on the first floor, with mainly temporary exhibitions on the

Cours Masséna is the setting for Antibes' picturesque market place

floor above. It is worth setting aside at least an hour for this museum.

The visitor, exhausted or enlivened, now has two main options. One is to return to the Cours Masséna and head back down the little hill through ancient buildings to the Old Port. The other is to make the walk a long one, leaving by the western end of the Cours Masséna and wandering among the old and flower-bedecked streets that wind round, with many restaurants and little shops, towards the newer part of town. The rue James Close is known for its small shops, some trendy, some touristy; and this leads towards the place Nationale, where again there are restaurants and cafés. From the place Nationale, the rue de la République brings the walker finally to the place de Gaulle and a view of the broader and more regimentally laid out streets of new Antibes. A tidy step back to the port completes the circuit.

◆◆
BIOT

Biot offers the architectural charm of old Provence in a richly floral landscape. In the nearby Fernand Léger Museum, it also possesses one of the finest modern monuments of the Côte d'Azur.

The district produces a glowing crop of carnations, roses and mimosa, much of it for the perfumeries of Grasse. The town is set most attractively on a small hill rising in the centre of a valley, with busy, stonebuilt streets and 16th-century gates. One central street, the rue St Sébastien, runs right along the crest of the hill, leading the visitor past attractive boutiques and cafés to the place des Arcades, a narrow rectangle with shrubs in the middle and on each of its long sides a row of arches. Some of these are round, some pointed, and they are set, most attractively, at varying heights. Beyond the place des Arcades comes the church, just on the edge of the hilltop and entered by a steeply descending flight of steps. It has two 15th-century Nice school altarpieces; it is particularly worth seeing *Our Lady of Mercy* by Louis Bréa, with a red rosary in the Virgin's right hand and the Christ Child on her left arm. In this sweet composition, smaller figures pray all round the Virgin.

Biot possessed rich clay deposits and was formerly famous for its pottery. Today, rather more is made of the various local glassworks with their characteristic bubbly glass, mainly pale green and brown, and much more attractive than it sounds. Visitors can watch the various stages of production, including energetic glass-blowing by men in shorts and eye-shields. The main establishment is the **Verrerie de Biot,** just by the southeast exit from the town, and open daily except some holidays (tel: 93 65 03 00).

Another major attraction at Biot is **the Fernand Léger Museum.** The work of Fernand Léger (1881-1955) was celebrated in his lifetime and has latterly attracted even more attention. Many will be familiar with his progression, during a long career, from early Cubism to an instantly recognisable preoccupation with machinery. In his later years he moved on yet again to a warmer vision, still involving machinery but with human beings playing a greater part. In the flat and repetitive impersonality of his middle period, he displays a

Cagnes-sur-Mer is made up of three areas: Haut-de-Cagnes, Cagnes-Ville and Cros-de-Cagnes, set between the sea and hills

machine-based romanticism which influenced other artists and still has strong resonance today.

Léger spent much of his time at Biot and after his death his wife Nadia donated 350 of his works to the striking museum which she erected, and whose architect was André Svetchine from Nice. Léger's Cubist period is less well represented than his later styles but the whole amounts to a most impressive tableau of his development. In the grounds, there are large, bright sculptures following Léger designs and the façades of the building carry enormous mosaics, worked up from tiny Léger originals. The director of the museum, M. Baulquier, handled the painter's affairs for

many years and is the leading authority on his life. The museum is normally open all year round (closed Tuesdays), but visitors should check first (tel: 93 65 63 61).
Biot is 2½ miles (4km) inland between Antibes and Cagnes-sur-Mer.

◆
CAGNES-SUR-MER
Just to the west of Nice, immediately beyond the airport and the mouth of the River Var, Cagnes-sur-Mer is several different places rolled into one. Cros-de-Cagnes, the seaside strip, is full of neon lights and pizzerias, apartment blocks, ice-creams and sandy bodies (Villeneuve-Loubet, next stop towards the west, is just as bad, or worse, with one major development of immense apartment blocks which dominates many miles of coastline.)
Cagnes-Ville, just in behind Cros-de-Cagnes and still on level ground, is busy, populous and provincial – though no doubt it was considerably quieter in the days of Renoir (1841-1919). The great Impressionist painter spent his last years here and the villa he occupied – **Les Collettes** – is now a museum. It has little of his work but, despite contemporary encroachments, still retains considerable atmosphere and a number of memorabilia (closed Tuesdays, and mid-October to mid-November).
Haut-de-Cagnes, rising beside Cagnes-Ville, is a steep hill with castle and old town perched up on top. This, though touristy, is

The perfume industry based in Grasse grew with the fashion for perfumed gloves, started in the 16th century by the Medicis

by far the most interesting part of the whole. It has ancient, winding streets and ramparts, restaurants and nightlife. The castle belonged to the Grimaldi family from 1309 (see **Monaco**) and was converted in 1620 into a stylish chateau. It is now a museum (open daily except Tuesdays in winter; closed mid-October to mid-November). It possesses a delightful renaissance patio, interesting paintings and several rooms devoted to the history and uses of the olive tree.

◆
CAP D'ANTIBES
The Cap d'Antibes is a wooded cape extending out into the Mediterranean between Antibes and Juan-les-Pins. The

rich have extremely pleasant homes here, with lush gardens behind walls and hedges. Up on the highest point of the peninsula, close to the lighthouse, is the **Sanctuaire de la Garoupe,** a chapel crowded with votive offerings: mainly paintings, in popular style, done to give thanks for restored health or escape from mortal danger, in fulfilment of a vow or as a plea for divine assistance. These are curious, sometimes comical and often moving, with one aisle devoted to marine offerings, one to affairs ashore.

◆◆◆
GRASSE
Set back 12 / miles (20km) from the coast at a height of 1,000ft (305m), Grasse looks for all the world like a substantial old Provençal hill town. In fact, the Italian influence was strong here, and for a time it was a tiny

republic closely tied to Pisa. As late as the 19th century, the novelist Stendhal recorded in his journal that it was 'completely Genoese in character' — and complained of the smell of the manure heaps. Today, this very pretty little city, medieval at heart but with modern buildings growing up all round, is better known as the perfume capital of France, and therefore of the world. Protected by the Pre-Alps from the north, Grasse looks down towards the sea over a landscape of rolling hills — now extremely well populated. From the country all round come the millions and millions of blooms and blossoms used by the local perfume factories. The factories extract perfume 'essence' which is then sent off to Paris to be blended by the great perfume houses. Grasse has steep and winding alleys, a solidly handsome cathedral, lively markets and above all — seen best from the place du Cours and a pleasing square tucked away behind the cathedral — wide views down to the sea. Like many towns in the area, Grasse has its Napoleonic anecdotes. After landing at Golfe Juan in 1815 on his return from Elba, Napoleon set off inland and soon reached Grasse, but he appears to have feared resistance. By-passing the town, he bivouacked briefly near by, then set off again for Lyons and Paris on what is now known as the Route Napoleon. Britain's Queen Victoria wintered in Grasse on several occasions, staying in a hotel now long converted into apartments.

The height and comparative coolness of the town gave it a great reputation as a health resort, in summer as in winter. The **Provençal Art and History Museum** is housed in a building known as the 'Petit Trianon', a mansion in a narrow street, built by the sister of the revolutionary leader Mirabeau. She became, by marriage, the Marquise de Cabris. In the basement there is a most enjoyable display of Provençal ceramics, many of them from the Côte d'Azur and giving some taste of what was once traditional ware — rather bizarre yellowy-green work from Biot, delightful 18th-century *faïence* from Moustiers, adventurous pieces from Vallauris. For those with an interest in furniture and decor, there are appropriate period apartments on the ground floor. The museum also exhibits a newly assembled collection illustrating the history of the perfume industry. This sprang up in association with the local tanning industry, much encouraged by Catherine de'Medici. Scented gloves were the big product. In due course, though, a tax on leather drove out the tanneries, leaving the perfume producers behind.

Perfume Visit

Several **perfume factories,** preserving old methods of manufacture for the tourist industry, are open to the public. The nearest to the Provençal Museum is the **Maison Fragonard,** just at the top of the same street. It is named for the painter Fragonard, a son of Grasse. On the upper level

THE CANNES COAST

there is a museum of perfume bottles and much evocative apparatus. On the lower level, old methods of extracting perfume essence are demonstrated and explained in well-organised guided tours — no charge but an opportunity, not by any means an obligation, to buy perfume at the end.

In the old method of extraction, the most delicate flowers are laid on beds of specially prepared cold fat — mostly pork and beef — which little by little absorb their scent. The flowers are changed daily and when the fat is fully impregnated, it is washed with alcohol, which in turn absorbs the essence. This process is called maceration. Flowers may also be macerated with hot fat. Other, tougher flowers — among them lavender and orange blossom — can be steamed to extract their essence. The last step is laboratory distillation — in huge stills from an alchemist's wildest dreams. This separates the essence from the alcohol in which most of it is now carried. All kinds of animal products were also once in use, some as fixatives for scent. They included ambergris from whales, musk from Tibetan deer, civet from wild cats and even bits and pieces from the unfortunate Canadian beaver. These have now been replaced by artificial chemicals. In modern factories, artificial chemicals are also used to extract the flower essence. The most effective substances are volatile solvents such as benzine — meaning that the public is definitely not welcome in their vicinity.

Perfume factories require the service of a 'nose', an individual as specialised as a great wine master who can recognise a multitude of scents and create blends from them. The 'nose' sits at an organ-like console flanked by shelves containing thousands of bottles. He can work for only two hours at a stretch before his sense of smell begins to dull. Naturally, he is considered an extremely precious person.

Juan-les-Pins is best known for its lively nightlife, but its sheltered beach has added to its reputation as a year-round resort

The statistics of perfume production are formidable. Just one sequence may be sufficient: 1,100lbs (500 kilos) of jasmine flowers are required to produce 2lbs (1 kilo) of jasmine essence. Every 2lbs (1 kilo) of jasmine is made of 15,000 to 20,000 flowers, picked by hand.

The presence of the perfume industry combines with a lively cut-flower trade to ensure that Provence is a particularly prolific flower-growing area — and prolific in greenhouses, too. Frost occasionally nips the mimosa trees whose brilliant yellows otherwise make a glorious display in January and February; and a recent frost also damaged local orange trees.

The painter Fragonard (1732-1806) — his lusciously sensual style is very familiar — abandoned Grasse for Paris but returned for a year during the French Revolution, staying with a relative in a handsome, if severe, old villa. This is now the **Villa-Musée Fragonard,** rather short on original works by the master but with a number of interesting paintings by his sister-in-law, Marguerite Gérard. The villa is just a step from the Maison Fragonard.

The **Cathedral of Notre-Dame-du-Puy** is certainly worth the short walk back into the old town. Entry is by a lovely 18th-century double staircase; the largely 12th-century interior is distinguished by ruggedly massive columns and a number of fine paintings — three works by Rubens which arrived via Italy and a supposedly religious Fragonard.

Always, as one goes about one's visiting, there is the beautiful view down to the sea.

◆
JUAN-LES-PINS
As resorts go, this near-neighbour and dependency of Antibes is a bit of a loudmouth — surprisingly, since it butts right up against the hushed exclusivity of Cap d'Antibes itself. The beach, which is mainly parcelled into private zones, each with restaurants and umbrellas, reclining chairs and mattresses, is a cheerful mass of bodies, brown and pink. Some of the beach establishments have *pétanque* (Provençal bowls); there are little piers, boats and parascending. There are also masses of pizzerias and boutiques, though often these are far from cheap. At night Juan-les-Pins rings to the sound of discos. In *Tender is the Night,* that haunting novel of the Riviera published in 1939, F. Scott Fitzgerald wrote of 'the constant carnival at Juan-les-Pins, where the night was musical and strident in many languages'. He had in mind a sophisticated stridency, befitting the early impetus given to the resort by the American millionaire Frank Jay Gould. What Gould or Scott Fitzgerald would make of Juan-les-Pins today is anybody's guess.

◆
MANDELIEU/LA NAPOULE
La Napoule is an up-and-coming resort near the less-favoured Mandelieu, a largely industrial town a little inland. La Napoule looks eastwards towards

THE CANNES COAST

Cannes and westwards towards the Esterel massif. The marina is tucked in below an extravagantly turreted castle, the principal landmark of La Napoule. Between 1917 and 1937 the castle was restored and filled to bursting with his own exotic works by Henry Clews, an eccentric millionaire sculptor from the USA.
Open: July and August only. Guided tours (tel: 93 49 95 05).

◆◆
MOUGINS

Mougins is a short distance inland behind Cannes, prettily situated on its own individual hilltop among steep little hills so thickly covered with neo-Provençal villas as to be, in effect, Cannes suburbs. Mougins has a photographic museum and a church tower with fine views. In its ancient stone architecture and winding little streets, it is a typical hill village, though one that is largely given over to restaurants. It is particularly popular with local people for Sunday lunch (see **Restaurants,** below).

◆◆◆
ST-PAUL-DE-VENCE

Visited as much, at least, as Èze on the Moyenne Corniche, St-Paul-de-Vence, some 5 miles (8km) inland from Cagnes-sur-Mer, is still a remarkably attractive place. Seen from the approach road, it is a huddle of grey-brown roofs within grey ramparts, rising from true Provençal slopes with cypresses and olives, oranges and even, in this case, the odd

banana tree. The whole is topped with a stone tower; and there are tantalising views down towards the sea over lines of receding hills.

The old town proper is divided by a single main street, the rue Grande. There is an urn-shaped fountain and a mass of tourist shops, with one or two good art galleries and jewellery. The part of town to the right is most heavily visited, the rue Grande giving easy access to the ramparts on this side. High up on the left of the rue Grande comes the church, and then, beyond it, down towards the ramparts on the further side, come quieter streets, with caged songbirds and the sound of whitebait frying behind lace curtains. The church itself is immensely wide, stretching across three broad naves. It harbours sundry notable works of art in its deep darkness. These can be illuminated by putting coins in the appropriate slot in the *éclairage* machine, to the left on entry.

The Maeght Foundation is reached by a side-turn off the main road from the coast just before entry to St-Paul. It is often described as the finest of the many museums and galleries in the south of France which are devoted to modern art and artists. It is certainly extremely striking. The intention of Aimé Maeght, the Parisian art dealer who established it, was 'to encourage a love of contemporary art in all its manifestations'. He chose a Catalan architect, J.L. Sert, who created a series of galleries which seem to weave in and out

The ancient fortified village of Mougins, with its narrow, winding streets and restored buildings, sits on a hilltop near Cannes

of the surrounding pine woods, bringing nature and human construction into the most intimate relationship. Terraces, gardens and courtyards surround and penetrate the Foundation, vivid with works by Braque, Giacometti, Miró and others. The galleries are unusual inside as well. Each ceiling is half a barrel vault, cut off by a perpendicular wall of glass through which light floods in on the display. Chagall, Léger and Miró are all well represented. Many of the finest works seem to be from about 1910 to 1930, with a garden of sculptures by Joan Miró dating from the '60s.

◆◆ VALLAURIS

Vallauris is in three ways a Picasso town — in painting, sculpture and ceramics. It is not, it's only fair to say, a particularly attractive place. Its prettiest part is made up of a pair of little squares at the top of town. From these a long and fairly drab main street tilts gently down the hill. The streets to either side are undistinguished. But thanks to Picasso's contribution, Vallauris is definitely a place to visit.

It had long been a pottery town but by the 1940s the potteries were in decline. Picasso, on a visit from the coast, decided he liked the output of a potter named Georges Ramié and began to work with him, decorating pots and dishes made by Ramié and often also reshaping them into surprising and adventurous forms. These he then painted in a design relating to their new shape. The results were often beautiful and amusing. Many can be seen in the castle at Antibes; there are others in the **Madoura pottery showrooms** in Vallauris. This was Ramié's own pottery and it continues today to produce studio works and numbered reproductions of the Picasso originals. There are also fine black and white photos of Picasso at work. The Madoura pottery is in a handsome old Provençal building but it is a little more shrine-like in atmosphere than the active spirit of Picasso might have wished. The tourist potteries in the town mostly turn out unappealing work; puce coffee cups are the norm.

Picasso actually moved to Vallauris while the ceramic urge was on him; his stay lasted 10 years. During this period, he was invited by the town to decorate a deconsecrated chapel up by the two little squares at the top of the main street. The result was one of his most famous works, a complete interior entirely devoted to a single theme. This interior or painting – call it what you will – is entitled *War and Peace* and the building is now known, inappropriately, as the **National Picasso Museum**. The visitor first enters a handsome courtyard with a large plane tree, then passes through a large and airy stone-built antechamber. The chapel leads off this, in shape rather like a short section of an underground railway tunnel but blocked off at the far end. The walls and ceiling of this ancient barrel-vault are entirely covered with huge sheets of plywood, painted by Picasso, then bent over into position and fastened with plain screws. On the left hand side as you enter there are grim scenes of war and pestilence, with weapons, warriors and blood. These give

way, on the right hand walls, to complicated symbolic scenes of love and reconciliation. The end wall also bears an allegory incorporating a dove, a sprig of olive and a vision of unity among the human races. The whole is superficially crude and urgent, parts recalling Picasso's earlier anti-war painting, *Guernica*.

Outside, in one of the little squares, there stands a statue which for years was the centre-piece of Picasso's studio. It is a strange work, showing a man with a head like a Greek god or warrior, holding a sheep in his hands. The sheep's legs are all bunched up and the animal looks faintly embarrassed. It is all most surprising and enjoyable, including the noisy teenagers

Contemporary sculpture is on display in the courtyards of the Maeght Foundation (see p50), designed to promote modern art

whose football cannons off the statue.

◆◆◆
VENCE

Most people come to Vence to visit the Matisse masterpiece, the **Chapel of the Rosary,** out beyond the centre on the far side of a valley. The chapel is outstanding, one of the simplest, purest and most completely achieved works in the long career of this extraordinary painter, and one of the key religious works of our whole century. It is certainly a must. But those who miss the town itself do themselves a disservice. First, then, the town of Vence and its long history. Vence was a substantial tribal centre, then a Roman town, and after that, from early Christian times, the site of an important bishopric. Its most notable citizen was one Antoine Godeau, a 17th-century ladies' man, famous in youth for ugliness and wit and one of the most acute minds of his day. He became bishop of Grasse and Vence at the age of 30 but the two towns were reluctant to accept a sole religious leader. After years of strife he made his choice for Vence and during the rest of his life did much for the diocese. Apart from Godeau, Vence is famed for the size of the fine old ash tree in the **place du Frêne.** Moving from this small square into the old inner town, with its handsome gateways and surviving chunks of rampart, the visitor encounters real liveliness and some sense of an ancient community. In the **Poterie du Peyra,** the pretty place du Peyra

possesses one of the most agreeable ceramics shops in the area. The Romanesque cathedral is staunch and solid and the engagingly carved 15th-century choirstalls repay scrutiny. The English novelist D.H. Lawrence died in Vence in 1930.

Matisse, who had taken up residence in Nice in 1921, moved on in 1943 to Vence and here experienced a long illness. Though not himself of a religious inclination, he was nursed through to health by Dominican nuns. In gratitude, he designed, financed and decorated the **Chapel of the Rosary,** *la Chapelle de la Rosaire,* for them; and in doing so, he achieved, at the age of 80, a work of calm and harmonious spirituality.

The chapel is a small building let into the hillside just below the road. It is entered by a downward flight of stairs with detailing of doors and windows marked by the delightful irregularity of Matisse's vision. Within, there are white walls with black and white murals — their colour, or lack of colour, rather, is pure Dominican — flowing across *faience* tiles. Stained glass in blues and greens and yellows lets in coloured pools of light in daytime, at evening only a muted glow. The extremely sculptural altar is surmounted by tall candlesticks and a slender cross, every detail worked out by Matisse. A little gallery running behind the chapel shows how he reduced his designs to achieve the final simplicity of the murals.

Accommodation

The little road around the Cap d'Antibes peninsula leads past the chateau-like **Hôtel du Cap,** with a turn-off almost immediately down towards the **Eden Roc** restaurant and its few hotel rooms. Both places are patronised by politicians, film-stars and singers. The Eden Roc has a lovely position. It is set on a rock, and has wide views over the Golfe Juan towards Cannes. The gardens behind are lovely, too, with tall pale pines reaching for the sun, their trunks like slightly drunken eucalyptus.

Other hotels in the area:
Antibes:
Auberge Provençale, 61 place Nationale (tel: 93 34 13 24). Relatively inexpensive.
L'Étoile, 8 bd James-Wylie (tel: 93 61 47 24).
Le Mas Djoliba, 29 ave de Provence (tel: 93 34 02 48). Between town centre and beach, set in garden.
Mougins:
Moulin de Mougins, 1½ miles (2.5km) from Mougins on D3 (tel: 93 75 78 24). The four-star de luxe hotel which goes with the restaurant cannot pass without mention. Roger Vergé is the chef at the restaurant (see **Restaurants,** below).

Restaurants

A number of attractive restaurants are gathered in or near a small triangular 'square' in Mougins, the place de la Mairie. These include the **Restaurant aux Trois Étages** (tel: 93 90 01 46); **Le Feu Follet** (tel: 93 90 15 78) and **Le Relais à Mougins** (tel: 93 90 03 47). Roger Vergé's **L'Amandier de Mougins,** near the entry to the village (tel: 93 90 00 91), is a converted olive-oil mill with a fine reputation (and a boutique at ground floor level). **Le Moulin de Mougins,** 1½ miles (2.5km) away at Notre-Dame-de-Vie (tel: 93 75 78 24), with Roger Vergé as chef, is one of the great gastronomic ports-of-call of the whole Riviera. Some think it the greatest.

The visitor to St-Paul-de-Vence encounters several of the most interesting features of the town in two eating houses, just before entering the old town. First, on the left, comes the beautiful but slightly 'uppity' **Colombe d'Or Inn.** This was a favourite haunt of painters such as Signac, Bonnard and Soutine and still possesses many works of art. Visitors can lunch on a terrace in front of the handsome old building — but woe betide the visitor who wants the art without the lunch.

Next, in the shade of plane trees, there is a lovely *pétanque* pitch and behind that the **Café de la Place.** On the terrace here you can get a drink or a simple meal and the bar inside is just what a real, old-fashioned bar should be — a long strip of zinc on a hardwood counter, with long brass rail and a million bottles reflecting against mirrors. Old men gesticulate as they discuss the *pétanque* competition or *concours*.

There are one or two pleasant eating places on the west side of the ramparts in St-Paul. **Le Bougainvillier** is typical — floral and rather pricey.

THE NICE AND MONTE-CARLO COAST

A view of the glorious coastline, from Nice towards Villefranche

THE NICE AND MONTE-CARLO COAST

From Nice to Monte-Carlo in the state of Monaco and on again to Menton, almost on the Italian border, the coast is grand and dramatic and the land behind it equally splendid. It was in Nice that the Riviera experience began, and it is this stretch of coast which is most deeply imbued with the special history of the Riviera. Monaco has played almost as great a part as Nice; Menton, too, had its particular fame in the early days.

Much of the coast is so steep and awesome that the roads along it are themselves a major phenomenon – the original Corniche, a name familiar through the world. At the foot of the steepest stretch nestle the beautiful resorts of Beaulieu and Villefranche. Behind, high villages cling to crags. This section of the coast also boasts two of the luxurious little peninsulas that are such a feature of the Riviera – Cap Ferrat and Cap Martin. It is perhaps the true heartland of the Riviera.

THE NICE AND MONTE-CARLO COAST

NICE

For many of those who get to know it well, Nice is by far the most interesting of the Riviera towns. But its many and considerable attractions tend sometimes to be obscured by the zappy claims of St Tropez or the rival promises of wealth and glamour offered by Cannes and Monte-Carlo. Addicts of these resorts like to see Nice as a little dowdy, the dowager of the Riviera rather than the pace-setter. Nothing could be less appropriate. Nice has the energy and character of a big city, and a Mediterranean city at that; a full and independent intellectual and commercial life, and the liveliness and welcome of a resort. It is a proper place, mature and vivid, dignified and playful, flanking the edge of a wide, blue bay — the beautifully-named Baie des Anges or Bay of Angels — and offering every variety of experience. Because its beaches are shingle rather than sand, you turn to the city as much as to the sea for pleasure and diversion — and that, too, is just as it should be, given the strong character of Nice. The gaudy floats of its Lenten Carnival and the brilliant colours of its annual Battle of Flowers express some of the rich and occasionally brawling high spirits, the warm embrace of the real Nice.

Nice, of course, was like all the other Riviera towns, in being originally a winter resort, later appropriated for summer pleasures. With the growth of the modern conference habit it is now witnessing the return of winter visitors. But regardless of season, the first and one of the most striking images it offers is its long sea-front to the west, the world-famous promenade des Anglais. As its name suggests, the construction of this sea-front road was originally financed, as a walk or promenade, at the expense of English residents in the 1820s. It stretches away in creamy silhouette against the blue of sea and sky and retains a substantial number of major 19th-century and Edwardian buildings. Some of the original grand hotels still stand and ply their trade. The domed

Négresco and the plainer Westminster, now Westminster Concorde, remain symbolic of the first Riviera, fashioned by the wealthy and aristocratic. Passing on along the Nice front towards the east and Italy, the picture soon becomes more complicated and intriguing. The promenade des Anglais ends in a park where the River Paillon once met the sea. Today the river is a trickle mostly confined underground. Behind this park, known as the **Jardin Albert 1,**

Now the capital of the Riviera, Nice began life as a trading post on the route to Marseilles

stands a handsome red ochre square constructed in Italian style early in the 19th century. This is the **place de Masséna,** generally considered the centre of town. On the front to the east of the Jardin Albert 1 there are buildings of varying dimensions — including an ornate opera house, rear end to the sea — which effectively conceal from the sea the intricate alleys, the markets and churches, the tiny old-fashioned shops and modern art galleries of the 17th-century Old Town.

After this along the front comes a high hill — called **Le Château,** though it conspicuously lacks a castle. Next comes the Old Port, dug out as a deep water harbour in the 18th century. The Old Port, though agreeably fringed along its western arm by fish restaurants, is a serious, hard-working place, many of its buildings in handsome red ochre like the place de Masséna. It handles the Corsica car-ferry and concerns itself a great deal less than other resorts with yachts. Le Château itself was the Acropolis of the original Greek settlement, now lost under greenery and later bits and pieces. It did indeed once have a major castle, swept away by a British general (see **Natives and Foreigners,** below).

What actually still stands today along the front or immediately behind it has a past which informs and helps to shape an extremely entertaining present. As one moves back from the sea, the mixture becomes, if possible, even more interesting. The range includes not just

THE NICE AND MONTE-CARLO COAST

Open-air cafés can be seen on Le Château hill – but no castle

contemporary residential and industrial districts but also a Russian Orthodox cathedral and a single vast building on a hill, the one-time Hôtel Regina, used in different ways at different times by Britain's Queen Victoria and the great French painter, Henri Matisse.
In understanding the geography of the city, the first principle to grasp is that the Old Town under the lee of Le Château was contained on one side by the sea and on the other by the River Paillon. The old river-bed appears on the map as a broad swathe of green interrupted by public buildings and flanked by large avenues. It runs diagonally inland from the sea front and still acts as a dividing line. To its east lies the enchanting triangle of the Old Town, while on the

west side of the river-bed lies the area that was built up as a new town during the 18th and 19th centuries.

The Old Town

A visit to the Old Town could begin at the Jardin Albert 1, with a stroll down the rue St-François-de-Paule, effectively a 19th-century approach road with interesting shops and galleries. Here, too, is the front end of the **Opera House,** with its faintly tatty pink marble columns and stained glass, a rickety-looking wrought-iron awning and extremely elaborate wrought-iron lanterns. St-François-de-Paule then broadens into the **Cours Saleya,** one of the most interesting little areas of Nice. Here, on the seaward side, there are two parallel rows of small two-storey buildings, the near side on the Cours Saleya, the far side on the sea front. These two rows of buildings are known as Les Ponchettes. Their tops provide two flat terraces, one on either side of the small road between them. They are now considerably complicated by chimneys but it was here, during early days, that the evening promenade of Nice was held, the ladies sitting on benches or strolling in their fine dresses, the beaux passing admiringly among them along the terraces of Les Ponchettes. The Cours Saleya itself, once upon a time the biggest wholesale flower market of the area, is now a colourful and energetic mixed market of flowers, fruit and vegetables. The produce is breathtakingly fresh, with glistening lettuces, aubergines and gladioli and, depending on the season, the tender fluffy yellow of mimosa or the rich russets and browns of wild funguses gathered for the delectation of specialist eaters. In the evening the Cours Saleya is a place of restaurants and entertainment.

One opening, landwards, from the Cours Saleya reveals the pomp of the Palais de Justice. Soon after this, the cranny of the rue de la Poissonnière could lead the walker, with just a slight diversion to the left, to the cathedral of **Ste Réparata,** with its baroque interior. Alternatively, holding as straight as possible, the walker would pass, by way of other baroque churches and chapels, tiny squares and narrow defiles between tall houses, all hung about liberally with washing, to the rue Droite with its handsome Genoese-style **Palais de Lascaris** (see **What to see,** below). Most of the surrounding streets are far too narrow for vehicles, though one or two do venture in to make deliveries and seem invariably to get stuck. A miniature wooden tourist train threads its way through. Often, there are unexpected views up to the green of Le Château and the ever-moving glint of an artificial waterfall at its summit. There are delicious coffee smells and cooking smells all around, and masses of happenings and people — old ladies out shopping, students enjoying

Amid the luxury and wealth of modern Nice, the Old Town brings a welcome touch of character

THE NICE AND MONTE-CARLO COAST

themselves, tourists exploring and a sudden view of a little tea-house, its only customers Moroccans and Algerians. Many little pasta shops with Italian names and plentiful Italian restaurants serve as a reminder that the city was in fact under the Italian rule of the Dukes of Savoy for 500 years up to 1860. A glance at the local telephone book reveals that a great many residents have Italian family names.

The attempt to proceed as straight as possible soon brings one to the **place St-François,** with a pretty little morning fish market and a view out of the Old Town towards the New. Another short walk up from the fish market leads to the lively **place Garibaldi,** with swarming traffic and one of the most promising corner cafés in town. This marks the extreme edge of the Old Town.

The New Town

The place de Masséna is a good spot for starting a visit to the so-called New Town, which is itself becoming quite venerable. Two important streets run out of place de Masséna. One is the **rue Masséna,** roughly parallel to the sea-front. The other is the **avenue Jean Médecin.** Masséna and the rue de France are the centre of a pedestrian precinct, with pizza houses and a good bookshop, a few interesting shops of their own and one or two small streets leading off with numerous small, high class shops (see **Shopping,** below). The avenue Jean Médecin is the main high street, with jeans out on racks on the pavement,

jewellery shops and larger shopping complexes. The most impressive is the modern, air-conditioned **Nice Étoile.** It's a hurly-burly street, with crowds and plane-trees, the liveliness of the passers-by again making the point that Nice exists in full flow and full energy as a city in its own right. There is a great sense of animation, of a rich emotional life being conducted all around. An arrow shot due north from the Jardin Albert 1 on the sea-front would pass directly between the Old Town and the New. A tourist following the same path would arrive, a mile (1.6km) from the front, at the base of a large hill rising from the flat coastal plain on which the centre of the city stands today. Here, east of the main railway station, there is a cluster of huge old hotels, now converted into apartments. A short way up again, but set back from the main road up the hill, a low, flat modern building, standing in its own garden, houses one of the most extraordinary spectacles in Nice: the vast series of works on Biblical subjects painted by Marc Chagall and given to the city (see **What to see,** below). These paintings form the core of a beautiful and moving museum. Now the main road, the boulevard de Cimiez, climbs up and up again (bus or car is essential for this journey) till it turns at an angle in front of a yet larger building of the old style, marking the top of the long rise. This vast rococo slab of faded dignity and lost pretensions is the **Hôtel Regina,** also converted into flats. Queen Victoria

wintered here several times, and it was here, on the third floor, that Henri Matisse later had an apartment. There is a hilltop park just across from the Regina, with dark green shrubs and pollarded olive trees set out in straight lines. The Romans, who followed the Greeks to Nice, used this hilltop as the site of their settlement, rather than Le Château. The consequence for us is a set of Roman ruins to survey. In this park there also stands a large Italian villa containing a memorable collection of the works of Henri Matisse. The park itself is the site of the annual Nice Jazz Festival − which accounts for the sculpted busts of Lionel Hampton and Louis Armstrong

Russians reaching Nice via the railway after 1864 were served by the Russian Orthodox Cathedral

lurking among the bushes. Nor should the far side of the park be missed; for here there is a Franciscan monastery and museum with fine late medieval paintings and a garden which looks down over the valley of the Paillon far below − this part of it now industrialised − and away down to the sea and Le Château.

Returning towards town one might now divert to the **Russian Orthodox Cathedral,** built with the financial assistance of Czar Nicholas II shortly before the Russian revolution. It was intended to serve the needs of

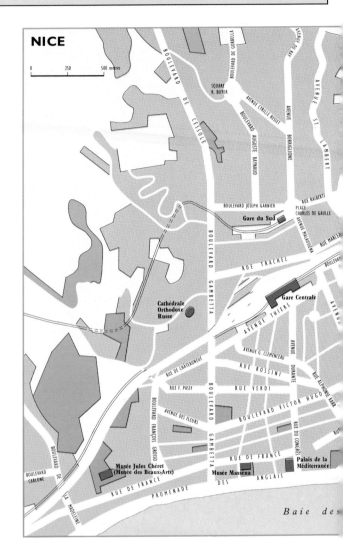

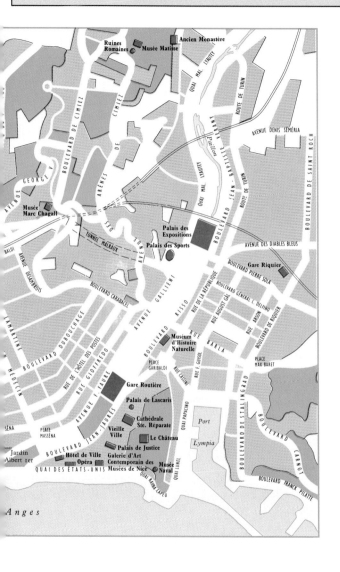

the aristocratic Russian colony who had made the Riviera a second home; and even today its green ceramic tiles and cluster of onion domes strike an exuberantly oriental note. It is floodlit in the evenings and there is a fine view of it from the westbound side of the inner city flyover (direction of Cannes), a true exotic among the slightly faded apartment blocks of this quarter of the city.

Two other areas are worth acquaintance and offer particular points of interest. About ten minutes' walk up the Paillon valley boulevards from the sea-front, a new arts and conference complex has lately been taking shape. The main buildings are the **Acropolis** conference centre, an octagonal theatre and a handsome **Museum of Modern and Contemporary Art** with four octagonal towers joined by bridges of glass and steel (see **What to see,** below). Together, these buildings form a kind of bridge between old and new Nice, and if some think they are short on the charm that lies so abundantly all around them, at least they are an affirmation that the city is alive and kicking. More traditional in feel, a mixture of buildings grander and humbler, with variety and change as you stroll along it, is the westward extension of the rue de France, one block behind the promenade des Anglais. It offers tantalising glimpses of the sea at every corner. The first real incident is the modern **Hôtel Elysée Palace,** rendered quite surprising by

Peering out at Nice: a permanent guest of the Hotel Elysée Palace, whose twin is in the opposite pillar

THE NICE AND MONTE-CARLO COAST

two vast sculpted ladies almost as tall as the building, squeezed into crannies on either side of the main entrance. Love them or loathe them, they are further evidence of the vigour of contemporary Nice. A little further along, the visitor reaches the Lycée Technique d'Hotelière et du Tourisme, hoping perhaps that its peeling paint is not an augury of things to come on the Riviera. Up behind it, and well signposted, stands a large and handsome villa, more a small-scale palace, which epitomises much of the history of the Riviera. It was commenced, in Genoese style, by a Russian princess. It was finished by an American millionaire. Today, under its twin names of **Jules Chéret Museum** and **Musée des Beaux-Arts** (Museum of Fine Arts), it houses one of those fine collections of paintings which have become such a feature of the south of France (see **What to see,** below).

Natives and Foreigners

Nice, like other spots on the Riviera, was settled by ancient Greek colonists from their western city of Marseilles. Its name is believed to derive from Niké, the Greek word for victory. The Romans came 200 years later, in about 200BC, creating a major settlement a little inland, up on the heights of Cimiez. After some centuries of post-Roman destruction and eclipse, Nice began to thrive again in the Middle Ages under the Counts of Provence. In 1388, thanks to a plot by one Jean Grimaldi, the governor, the city

passed, with great rejoicing, into the control of the Dukes of Savoy. It remained Savoyard – and, therefore, Italian – right up to 1860.

The city's greatest heroine is Catherine Ségurane. In 1538, Nice was besieged by the corsair Khaereddin Barbarossa. Catherine was in the act of delivering food to the soldiers when the attackers came swarming over the ramparts of Le Château. Setting down her basket, she killed several personally, then grabbed a standard and led a counter-attack, concluding the affair with a celebrated 'moonie' from the ramparts.

In 1706 Le Château was captured and razed to the ground by the English Duke of Berwick, serving with Louis XIV. Napoleon Bonaparte spent two turbulent periods in Nice, in 1794 and 1796, and the Napoleonic Marshal Masséna sprang from this city, whose main square and pedestrian shopping street now bear his name. Garibaldi, the Italian general, was born here in 1806 and, as we have seen, has also given his name to a square. In modern times, Nice has been ruled by a tough but enterprising right-wing dynasty, the Médecin family, with father and son successively holding the post of mayor. The main shopping street, Jean Médecin Avenue, is named for the father of Jacques, the present incumbent. A tour of the town's posters will reveal that the cult of personality is alive and well. Foreigners, of course, have played a great part in the evolution of contemporary Nice. The English novelist Tobias Smollett spent ten months here in 1763 and was followed by a growing number of British grandees. By 1822, they were constructing the promenade des Anglais and dominating the New Town to the west of the River Paillon. Nietzsche and Berlioz both enjoyed creative spells in Nice and wrote about their experiences amusingly. Queen Victoria came too and, in due course, the Russian aristocrats, for whom the cathedral was constructed. For all of these people, Nice was predominantly a winter resort and so it mostly remained until, in the years after World War II, northern Europeans turned in their millions to the summer sun.

WHAT TO SEE

◆
CATHEDRAL OF STE RÉPARATA
place Rossetti, Old Town.
A baroque building from the 17th century, with energetic marble and plasterwork inside.

◆◆◆
CHAGALL (MARC) MUSEUM
ave Dr Menard.
Marc Chagall was born in 1887 into a poor Jewish family in Russia and finished his long career on the Côte d'Azur. For him the Bible was 'not the dream of a people . . . but that of humanity' and here, between 1954 and 1967, he created two great cycles of paintings on biblical themes. The airily modern Chagall Museum, which opened in 1973, was intended

principally as a show-case for these huge and luminous works, full of the brilliant colours, the joy, the sense of suffering, the simplicity of vision that gives such deep delight to his admirers. There are many other, smaller works by Chagall on display, and fine Chagall stained glass in the museum's lecture and concert room.
Closed: Tuesdays.

◆◆◆
JULES CHÉRET MUSEUM
(Museum of Fine Art),
33 ave des Baumettes.
This is another great treat, partly because of the building, but also because of the varied collection of paintings. These start with Italian primitives and range right through into the 20th century. The Impressionists are well represented with work by Monet and Sisley's *Alley of Poplars,* a key Impressionist landscape. There are works by Raoul Dufy, pretty pastels by Jules Chéret himself and intriguing, sickly scenes by the Nice painter, Gustav-Adolf Mossa. This museum is not to be missed.
Closed: Mondays, and first two weeks of November.

◆
LASCARIS PALACE
rue Droite.
A 17th-century palace in Genoese style in the narrow streets of the Old Town. Handsome façade, grand staircase, paintings and tapestries. Guided tours only. Starting point for tours of the Old Town.
Closed: Mondays and November.

◆◆
MASSÉNA MUSEUM
65 rue de France.
In a palatial turn-of-the-century building, the Masséna Museum houses a mixed collection of Napoleonic souvenirs and works of art. There are religious paintings from the remarkable 15th-century Nice School by Jacques Durandi and Louis Bréa.
Closed: Mondays and two weeks in November.

◆◆◆
MATISSE MUSEUM
164 ave Arènes-de-Cimiez.
A large villa in Cimiez provides a tour of the translucent career of Henri Matisse (1869-1952), from the first explosions of Fauvist joy and colour early in the century to the untroubled serenity and flowing lines of his later work. In Nice, from 1921, he produced an unbroken stream of masterpieces, with some of the most delightful still to be seen here in Cimiez. Check before visiting, however (tel: 93 81 59 57). The museum shut some time ago for repairs; a Roman aqueduct was discovered in the basement and now the closure seems likely to be prolonged. On the same site, appropriately, is the Archaeological Museum, with exhibits from Cimiez as well as round about.

◆◆
MUSEUM OF MODERN AND CONTEMPORARY ART
Le Paillon, opposite ave St Jean Baptiste.
A brand new building whose octagonal towers are linked by

The Chéret Museum, an 1878 villa built for Princess Kotschoubey

glassed-in walkways, the Museum exhibits works of the 20th-century Nice school – the painters and sculptors who flourished here in the '60s and '70s, making Nice second only to Paris in French art.
Artists like César and Arman, with their compressed cars and endlessly repeating violins, were offering as precise a comment on the consumer society as American contemporaries Warhol and Liechtenstein, and are now held in high repute.

Accommodation
Expensive:
Négresco, 37 promenade des Anglais (tel: 93 88 39 51). With the Hôtel de Paris in Monte-Carlo a close runner-up, this has to rank as the great establishment of the Riviera. Built 1913, declared a national

THE NICE AND MONTE-CARLO COAST

monument in 1974. Amazingly plush without being repulsive, modern comforts and impeccable service alongside period pieces and works of art — not to mention the baccarat crystal chandelier in the Salon Royal, weighing in at a ton of glass. Definitely a palace — even Britain's Queen Elizabeth has stayed here.

Westminster Concorde, 27 promenade des Anglais (tel: 93 88 29 44). Another in the great wedding cake tradition, now under Concorde group management.

Méridien, 1 promenade des Anglais (tel: 93 82 25 25). This luxury hotel on the front, even more central than the Négresco and Westminster, is the modern alternative. Good and friendly service, much used by business people.

Reasonable:

La Malmaison, 48 boulevard Victor-Hugo (tel: 93 87 62 56). Traditional decor and attractive rooms.

Continental Masséna, 58 rue Gioffredo (tel: 93 85 49 25). Cheaper:

Relais de Rimiez, 128 ave de Rimiez (tel: 93 81 18 65). Quiet hotel on hill 10 minutes by car behind centre.

Ibis, 350 boulevard Corniglion Molinier (tel: 93 83 30 30). Close to airport, its merit is comparative cheapness.

Nightlife

After a drink on the Cours Saleya, followed by dinner at **Safari,** 1 Cours Saleya (tel: 93 80 18 44) or **La Petite Maison Ferrier,** corner rue de l'Opéra and rue St-François-de-Paule

(tel: 93 92 59 59), all in the same area, the smartest folk move on to the **Camargue,** 6 place Charles-Félix (tel: 93 85 74 10). **Findlatter's,** 6 rue Léponte, is for the thrusting young, chic punk being the dominant style.

Restaurants

Nice is a good place for food. It is a meeting point for Provençal and Italian cooking and has given its own name to various dishes — notably *salade niçoise* and *boeuf nçois.* There is plenty of fresh fish on offer, along with *socca* and *pan bagnat* in stand-up restaurants and stalls. The main restaurant areas are the Cours Saleya, the Masséna pedestrian zone, the Old Town proper and the harbour area. But there are plenty of other acceptable eating places almost everywhere, big city style. All kinds of wine are available, of course, but in the cheaper restaurants, locals drink the local rosés.

The pride of the expensive and grand restaurants are:

Le Chantecler, in the Négresco Hotel, 37 promenade des Anglais (tel: 93 88 39 51). Its new young chef Dominique Le Stanc has progressed through Monte-Carlo and Èze with the public adulation that would surround a film star elsewhere. Time will tell what he can make of this most famous of Riviera restaurants.

Closed: November.

L'Univers, 54 bd Jean Jaurès (tel: 93 62 32 22). Rather large but one of several top class fish restaurants in town (Coco Beach, out past the Old Port and keeping as close to the sea as possible, has a tremendous reputation and tremendous prices).

Traditional Nice food is available at:

Au Chapon Fin, 1 rue de Moulin (tel: 93 80 56 92). Father and older son undertake the hearty Provençal cookery, mother and younger son serve it up in this old-fashioned little restaurant with sweetly decorated plaster ceilings.
Closed: Sundays and January.

Lou Balico, 20 ave St Jean Baptiste (tel: 93 85 93 71). Much talked about, thanks to the eccentricities of its owner, Adrienne. The kind of place where they let you in if they like

The Masséna pedestrian area is busy with cafés and restaurants

you and everybody has to sing.

Lou Pistou, 4 rue de la Terrasse in the Old Town. A slip of a restaurant, informal and tasty, not really a place for booking. Cookery and local gossip by Isabelle and Michel.

Nice is strong on cafés and bars – good places to sit, indoors and out. In summer, tables are set out in the Cours Saleya and the little cathedral square in the Old Town. The **Scotch Tea House** (ave de Suède et Gustav-V), with tartan carpets and framed posters of modern art, sells porridge and cornflakes at any time of day. It's a pleasant place to rest one's feet, entirely superior to **Pam-Pam,** diagonally opposite across the Jardin Albert 1, a fashionable but tacky joint with Latin American music and drinks with fancy names.

THE NICE AND MONTE-CARLO COAST

For a touch of old-fashioned splendour, with balcony and dark-wood panelling, what else but a cocktail in the **Négresco** bar? For oysters and a good vantage point, **Le Grand Café de Turin** in the place Garibaldi.

Shopping

Nice has every class of shop. The avenue Jean Médecin is a prosperous high street with department stores and a pair of shopping malls – the Nouvelles Galeries and the Nice Étoile. The smarter shops are down by the pedestrian rue Masséna, off the place de Masséna. The rue Masséna itself is crammed with a range of boutiques and fast eateries and most of the elegance is concentrated in little streets pointing in the general direction of the sea. Take the rue Paradis, for instance. Here Nereides, on the corner, sells the most extravagant costume jewellery – large, shiny, ornate bangles, necklaces and earrings. There is Façonnables, a smart and up-to-the-minute men's shop with aspirations indicated by the British Royal coat of arms over its door. Not many doors away, Gladys Falk stocks clothes ranging from rather old-fashioned smocked rompers and dresses to elegant little ensembles of jackets and skirts. Nearby Alain Figaret sells shirts for men and women in a variety of tastes and styles.

A street well worth inclusion on any round of the shops is the rue St-François-de-Paule. Auer, just opposite the Opera House, sells jams and candied fruit and cakes. Its very pretty interior has rococo counters and there is a small tea room tucked away behind. The Alziari olive oil shop is on the Opera side of the road, a true specialist house in all that is associated with the olive. Alziari tins are old-fashioned and lovely; the oil is excellent. Part of the pleasure of shopping in Nice is that locals use these shops as well.

Nice has many art galleries. Art'nold, also in St-François-de-Paule, specialises in less well-known contemporaries and offers painting sessions for children. The Galerie Ferrerro, 24 rue de France and 2 rue de Congrès, is very up-market, with major works by modern Nice School artists and others. These are just two examples; in the Old Town in particular there are many smaller galleries to be discovered and enjoyed.

Special Events

Nice is famous for its Carnival fortnight in the pre-Lenten period running up to Mardi Gras (Shrove Tuesday) and its Battle of Flowers (main day, Ash Wednesday). This is a time of processions and street life with elaborate floats, outsize and often grotesque figures on parade, and plenty of people pelting plenty of others with cut flowers. All very heady, not to say intoxicating.

The Nice Jazz Festival, closely linked to the jazz festival in New Orleans, is in July, in Cimiez. There are three different stages, all outdoors, and visitors can rotate among them on the same ticket. Top-class international musicians.

Monte-Carlo, laid out on the headland of Monaco since 1828 and from the 1850s a gambling centre

MONACO AND MONTE-CARLO

Monaco is the ancient and miniature principality of the Grimaldis, ruled over at present by Prince Rainier III, husband of the late Grace Kelly, father of Caroline, Albert and Stephanie. Monte-Carlo is the stumpy little headland in the principality, not even named till the last century, on which the world's most famous casino stands. The casino itself is surrounded by luxurious hotels, the historic Café de Paris and some of Europe's grandest little shops. While in theory Monte-Carlo is merely one incident on the map of Monaco, in practice, of course, it is Monte-Carlo which has given the principality much of its fame. That and the fact, extraordinary but true, that Monegasque citizens pay no income tax.

Monaco has sea in front of it and mountain rising steeply behind. The most dramatic point in the principality's high backdrop is an enormous and looming crag known as the Dog's Head or **Tête de Chien.** Directly under the Tête de Chien, a high, flat promontory shaped like a curling shrimp stretches a good way out into the sea. On the landward side, this peninsula is cut off by the extravagant crenellations of Prince Rainier's palace.

Beyond the palace, on the seaward portions of the headland, stands an old town with narrow streets, a cluster of administrative buildings, a late 19th-century cathedral — burial place of Princess Grace — and an Oceanographic Institute which is impressively grand and grey. This promontory, often called **le Rocher,** is the heart of the old principality. It forms the western side of an almost rectangular bay. The whole of this is a harbour and it provides moorings for some of the most spectacular yachts in the

Mediterranean. Here one may see private motor vessels which really could be small cruise liners. Behind the port comes an area built up in the late 19th century and called **la Condamine.** Beyond the harbour, forming the eastern side of the rectangle, rises the much smaller promontory of Monte-Carlo. While le Rocher, on the western side, is basically a high rock with buildings on its upper surface, Monte-Carlo is a steep-sided hill with roads and buildings climbing up in terraces. In Monte-Carlo, too, however, the critical area is really just the top of the hill with its extravagant buildings from the *belle époque,* the final years of the last century and the start of this one. The casino, resplendent with towers and period roofscape (and also containing an opera house and cabaret), is just about on the summit. Beneath it on the seaward side, supported on pillars, is a huge new conference centre. Inland from the casino, at the upper level, is an open space with gardens. These are flanked on one side by the newly refurbished **Café de Paris,** containing restaurant and a gaming house. Opposite is the **Hôtel de Paris,** full of *belle époque* splendours and magnificent restaurants — and boasting, 50ft (15m) down in solid rock, the world's largest

The present Casino at Monte-Carlo dates from 1879, but the original enterprise got underway in 1856

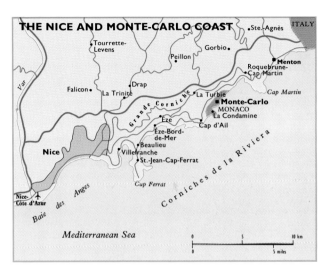

THE NICE AND MONTE-CARLO COAST

hotel wine-cellar. Tucked behind the Hôtel de Paris is a tiny street containing nothing but shops with legendary names and then another little open space, the **Square Beaumarchais,** backed by the Hermitage, another *belle époque* hotel.

All this is the real core of the area, though a handful of newer luxury hotels, among them the Mirabeau and Loews, round off the splendours of Monte-Carlo to the east.

The whole of the assemblage — Prince Rainier's rock, la Condamine and Monte-Carlo just beyond — is now ringed in and strait-jacketed by high-rise apartment blocks and other buildings, desperately taking advantage of every inch of soil and rock to provide living space for a population of 27,000. These are mostly French and Italians but with some 4,500

Monegasques. So tiny is the principality that much of what appears to be Monaco or Monte-Carlo is technically on French soil as the small, dense conurbation surges up the mountainside. At sea-level to the east there are the man-made beaches of Larvotto. To the west, beyond le Rocher, there is a small, packed zone with housing, industry and a major sports stadium, all on artificial land. This area is called Fontvieille.

And that makes up the little Principality of Monaco, home of Monte-Carlo.

Quick Riches

Monte-Carlo's own rise to fame was swift and extraordinary and did not begin until the 1850s. At this point the principality was in the process of losing to France its long-held fiefs of Roquebrune and Menton, rich in olive oil and lemons. As a result of this loss, Monaco went suddenly and spectacularly broke. Gambling was forbidden in France and the newly impoverished principality decided to take advantage of its only asset − independence − by turning itself into a gambling haven. Communications by land and sea, however, were so terrible that the first gambling house was a flop.

In this emergency the Grimaldi of the day, Prince Charles III, brought in a French entrepreneurial wizard named François Blanc, already famed for his casino in Bad Homburg, to set up a new resort for gambling and pleasure. This was established on the hill now named Monte-Carlo in honour of the prince; the company was disarmingly christened the Société des Bains de Mer − the Sea-bathing Society. After 120 years, it is still alive and well and better known by its initials, SBM. The company continues to control the Casino and other gambling spots in the principality, all the grandest of the belle époque hotels, the Café de Paris and a host of other buildings and activities. It is the main employer in the principality.

It was the arrival of the railway in 1868 which allowed François Blanc and Monte-Carlo to succeed so spectacularly. The railway brought into Monaco the wealthy and aristocratic visitors who had already made the fortunes of Nice and Cannes. They came in amazing numbers. By the 1870s, Monte-Carlo was receiving some 150,000 people

a year, well on the way to the mass tourism of modern times. Visitors included the royalty and nobility of many countries, their friends and mistresses and other admirers. The 'man who broke the bank at Monte-Carlo' was an English confidence trickster named Charles Wells; he performed his feat in 1887. The great wealth accumulated in the late 19th century led at that time to the reconstruction of the cathedral on le Rocher. Rich beyond the wildest dreams of his forebears, Prince Albert I of Monaco at the turn of the century voyaged the oceans of the world in quest of scientific discoveries. These were housed in the purpose-built **Oceanographic Institute** which is today so great a feature of Monaco. The casino itself was rebuilt in the highest style of the belle époque by Charles Garnier, architect of the Paris Opera House. An opera house was installed within the casino complex at the same time. The opera enjoyed huge success and Monte-Carlo also became the home of Diaghilev's Ballet Russe. Though somewhat interrupted by World War I, Monte-Carlo and Monaco remained the last word in luxury, expensive art and elegance right up to 1939. The principality emerged from World War II once again impoverished. An extra problem was that gambling had by now become legal in France; many rival casinos were flourishing or soon to flourish on the Côte d'Azur. In 1949 Prince Rainier III succeeded to the title at the age of 25. Since then,

MONACO AND MONTE-CARLO

Founded in 1910, Monaco's Oceanographic Institute is a museum of marine curiosities and a centre for underwater studies

Monaco has gradually won back its former splendour and re-established itself at the centre of international attention. This is partly because of Rainier's energetic building programme. The newly-won building space in Fontvieille and at the seaward tip of Monte-Carlo have enabled the 'Builder Prince' to diversify Monaco's economy. Along with Cannes and Nice, Monaco is now a major Mediterranean conference centre, equipped as much for business travel as for conventional tourism. Banking and the real estate business contribute handsomely to the principality's coffers. Industrial undertakings in Fontvieille include cosmetics, plastics and food-processing. Monaco gains its public wealth mainly from value added tax and is proud to boast that only 4 to 5 per cent of its income is derived from gambling.

There is no doubt that Monaco moved back on to the world stage partly because of Prince Rainier's marriage to the American actress Grace Kelly in 1956. Though sometimes regarded as too transatlantic an influence, Princess Grace indentified herself with Monaco and its people and together she and the prince brought their tiny territory into a new era. Princess Grace's tragic death in an accident on a twisting mountain road in 1982 still casts a long shadow over this bustling, successful and energetic little place.

As regards visiting, Monaco differs from most other towns on the Côte d'Azur in being dedicated almost exclusively to the wealthy. Eighty per cent of hotels are four-star or four-star *de luxe* and there is a cheerful assumption among the inhabitants that you will find it delightful to contribute to their good fortune. Most restaurants are expensive. Even entrance fees to museums and other places of interest seem considerably steeper than elsewhere. On the other hand, it is an exceedingly interesting place for which you may well be willing to pay a premium. Day trips are one solution and there is plenty to be seen and enjoyed during a visit of just a few hours. But many may find it worthwhile to dig deep in their

The Grottes de l'Observatoire caves form part of the Jardin Exotique, where the early history of human habitation can be traced

pockets and stay in style for a night or two to get the atmosphere — one of luxury and enclosure and surprising separateness from the rest of the Riviera. There is plenty of police presence in Monaco and it is one of the few places, perhaps the only one, where it is both safe and acceptable to wear expensive jewellery in the street at night. There are luxurious (paying) beaches. Quite apart from the gambling and smart shopping (see below) the whole place is sports mad, with the annual Monte-Carlo Rally, the Grand Prix and a soccer side which topped the French league in 1987 and regularly does well in Europe. Boris Becker and other tennis stars live in Monaco; there is a spectacular country club with many courts. Also, high on the mountain in French territory, is a golf club with amazing views. The **Sporting Club de Monaco** is a building down on the sea's edge to the east of Monte-Carlo where the grandest gala dinners and other international events are held. Some of the rich inhabitants here look astonishingly fit — a tribute, if any were needed, to the restorative powers of leisure.

The Grimaldi Story

Caves and rock shelters in Monaco and on the mountainside above were inhabited in the prehistoric period. The Phoenicians arrived early in historical times. Later on there came a tribe called the Monoeci who have supposedly given their name to the principality; it was also called Port Hercules after a temple dedicated to the hero.

From the 12th century, the territory was under Genoese control, and during the course of faction-fighting between Genoese Guelfs and Ghibellines it came under the lordship of the Grimaldi family. Legend has the first of the Monaco Grimaldis entering the castle with his men in 1297 disguised as a monk, then throwing off his cloak to confound all about him. This is the origin of the monks with sword on the Grimaldi shield.

By 1308, Monaco was definitively under the control of the Grimaldis and has remained so ever since. They were a large and important family who also owned Antibes, the castle at Cagnes, Grimaud and other places and it was a Grimaldi who betrayed Nice to the Dukes of Savoy in 1388. At various times their little territory of Monaco passed under foreign domination but always bobbed up again with some sort of independence. On two occasions the male line has died out, but the princes who married into the family took the Grimaldi name. The Grimaldi story is full of deeds of blood and heroism, with the emergence, during the 19th century, of a more modern approach. Even so, the ruler still retains powers that are close to absolute. The loyalty of subjects is amply assured, however, by an agreement that the principality will become French, should the line of the Grimaldis perish.

WHAT TO SEE

◆◆
CAFÉ DE PARIS
Monte-Carlo.
This handsome building, recently refurbished and equipped with a modern range of amenities, specialises in American games — black jack, craps, etc — and in one-armed bandits, politely described as slot-machines.

◆◆◆
THE CASINO
Monte-Carlo.
The Casino is the central showpiece of Monte-Carlo. Its unique atmosphere derives from the hushed and serious demeanour of the players gathered round the tables, from the lavish decorations of the *belle époque* and from subsequent additions and refurbishments. Several rooms in the casino reopened in 1989 after repair and restoration. There are high ceilings decorated with painted medallions and stained glass panels, with an emphasis on wispy ladies floating in a floral atmosphere, the mildest suggestion of naughtiness and plenty of gilding. The Casino specialises in traditional gambling, featuring, among other games, much roulette and baccarat. Players sit or stand at the tables, and observers lean on padded rails at elbow height around the end. A 'chef' sits at the head of each table. The chefs are neat and watchful men whose feet, encased in patent leather shoes, rest on cross-bars between the legs of their high chairs. The croupiers, too, are watchful, helping allocate counters to the spaces intended by the players, raking them in afterwards with little pushers on sticks like miniature brooms. Observers eddy from table to table, congregating where the big money is in action. Most of today's players are Italian, in sharp contrast to the English and even Russian atmosphere of earlier periods. Entry on production of passport or identity document. On the seaward side of the Casino, there is an elaborate terrace with fine views of the coast. From here, the casino building can also be seen at its grandest.

◆
CATHEDRAL OF ST NICOLAS
le Rocher.
A short step from the palace, this neo-Romanesque cathedral with a mildly Byzantine air was built in 1875 on the ruins of the old church of St Nicolas, in rather chilly white stone. Princess Grace's tomb is in the stone floor of the inner side of the ambulatory at the rear. There are two fine paintings of the 15th-century Nice School by Louis Bréa (note especially the eight-panel altarpiece dedicated to St Nicolas, in the ambulatory shortly before Princess Grace's tomb).

◆
CHAPEL OF THE MISERICORD
A handsome, if severe, 17th-century building opposite the Mairie or Town Hall. The pretty interior reveals the high reach of the walls and shallow vaulting. In an illuminated glass case is a dolorous image of Christ, which is carried through

Princess Grace, a star who became a royal, is fondly remembered

the streets under a canopy on Good Friday. Also, in a case of its own, is quite a large bone formerly belonging to Ste Dévote, virgin, martyr and patroness of Monaco.

◆
LOEWS HOTEL
Monte-Carlo.
There is a large and modern casino here on the ground floor under a glittering ceiling which reflects the green of the gaming tables and the slot-machines. Busy and active. Free entry.

◆
MONTE-CARLO STORY
A multi-slide audio-visual reprise of Monaco's history, this could serve as an interesting

introduction to the area. The display is in an auditorium linked to the car park of Les Pêcheurs.

◆◆◆
OCEANOGRAPHIC INSTITUTE
le Rocher.
This is the star exhibit of le Rocher, even more interesting than the palace. The lowest floor contains a fine aquarium. A series of tanks holds underwater creatures of the Mediterranean — not just fish, but also huge octopuses with the sad eyes of elephants and moray eels with dog-like heads too small for their thick bodies. Tropical sea-life is represented by fish of extraordinary form and colour and by such fascinating displays as a living cross-section of a Pacific atoll. The central floor shows whales' skeletons,

Changing of the Guard at the Prince's Palace, built on the site of a 13th-century fortress

deep-sea diving devices for oceanographic exploration and other pieces of modern wizardry. The top floor contains modern exhibits on the behaviour of the ocean and much of the huge collection assembled by Prince Albert I, its thousands of drawers and neat glass cases a tribute to the 19th-century spirit of inquiry.

◆◆
THE PRINCE'S PALACE

The best approach to the palace is on foot up the steep ramp from the place d'Armes in la Condamine; or by bus; or by driving to the car park, then taking the lift. From the open space in front of the ornate palace, there are fine views down on the east side over the harbour and Monte-Carlo and westwards over Fontvieille and Cap-d'Ail. Palace guards stride

back and forth in operatic uniforms past cannons and cannonballs. Changing of the Guard takes place at 11.55am, with seagulls and sparrows competing for attention. Guided tours (July to September) take visitors through a palace whose oldest portions are 13th century, with other parts from the 15th and 16th centuries. There were modifications to living quarters and the external appearance late in the 19th century, in gothic revival style. Fine paintings, carpets and furniture can be seen, and also in the palace is the Museum of Napoleon and Palace Archives. This possesses Napoleon's own razors and the tricorn hat he lost at the battle of Marengo in 1800. There are masses of coins and medals and prints of ancient Monaco. Note also the handsome headquarters of Carabiniers on the far side of the square opposite the palace entrance. Near by a waxworks museum, **Historial des Princes de Monaco,** shows scenes from the princely progress. These could not be described as very subtle but they are quite jolly and informative.

Open: all year, except Mondays in winter and January, early February.

◆
TROPICAL GARDENS (JARDIN EXOTIQUE) AND ANTHROPOLOGICAL MUSEUM
The tropical gardens are basically a fine collection of cacti and succulents, extraordinary in shape and virulent with spikes and bristles, prickles and spears, and vegetable sword-blades. They grow on what is virtually a cliff with steps leading to the mouth of a cave inhabited in prehistoric times. There are guided tours of the cave. Fine views take in le Rocher, the palace and Fontvieille. The Anthropological Museum is also within the gardens and reminiscent, though on a smaller scale, of the Oceanographic Institute with its collector's zeal. You learn a good deal about early Mediterranean man and his environment, and there are pictures of Prince Albert I as huntsman, slaughtering large beasts in various parts of the globe. The gardens are situated on a slope above the town and are well signposted by road.

Accommodation
Beach Plaza, 22 ave Princesse Grace, a modern hotel with excellent beach facilities on eastern side of Principality. Trust House Forte, convenient for business people, agreeable for the active, not so much personality.
Hôtel Hermitage, square Beaumarchais (tel: 93 50 67 31). This is another belle époque palace, with vast, old-fashioned rooms appointed to the highest modern standards. The Winter Garden and Belle Époque Restaurant should in any event be on one's list of sights. The former is really just a two-storey rectangular room with balcony and stained glass dome but the effect is marvellously light and airy, the stained glass dome a beautiful sun-flower pattern.
Hôtel de Paris, place du Casino (tel: 93 50 80 80). Right across the road from the Monte-Carlo casino and with views from the higher floors back towards Italy and on to le Rocher, the Hôtel de Paris occupies about the most promising position on the Riviera. It is also wonderfully grand, redolent with the story of an earlier way of life. The hotel has a magnificent wine cellar, not open to the public, with long underground alleyways for different classes of drink. The champagne 'alley' seems to express the spirit of the place most eloquently, though there are many splendid wines going back to the 1920s and brandy hogsheads, topped up every two years, which originated early in the 19th century. There are even a few bottles dated 1805 and 1809. Altogether the

cellar has some 250,000 bottles, mainly of wine.

Reasonable:

Hôtel le Siècle, 10 ave Prince Pierre (tel: 93 30 25 56). Comfortable and much appreciated by its clients.

Le Balmoral, 12 ave de la Costa (tel: 93 50 62 37). Name and address — Scots royal and Italian — sum up much of older Monte-Carlo. Some rooms with fine harbour view. Well positioned for Monte-Carlo centre if you can walk up a short hill.

Cheaper:

Terminus, 9 ave Prince Pierre (tel: 98 30 20 70).

Hôtel de la Poste, 5 rue des Oliviers (tel: 93 30 70 56).

Nightlife

The top night spot is still **Jimmy'z** (tel: 93 30 71 71) in the Monte-Carlo Sporting Club. Essentially, it's a smart disco where, as well as the younger crowd, distinctly mature ladies can be seen in sequins along with their well-heeled escorts. Prince Albert sometimes attends. Other venues include:

The Living Room, 7 avenue des Spélugues (tel: 93 50 80 41). Right in the middle of Monte-Carlo, offers piano bar and disco until dawn, more fashionable than brash.

Noroc, 7 rue Portier (tel: 93 25 09 25). Very fashionable among the young, was opened originally by Mariana Simionescu, Monte-Carlo personality and one-time wife of tennis champion Bjorn Borg.

Restaurants

Just as 80 per cent of Monaco's hotel rooms are at the top of the

scale, so restaurants, too, tend to the grand and expensive. Caviar beluga is the foodstuff of Monte-Carlo; champagne, preferably pink, is the symbolic drink. Here is a selection of tip-top restaurants and a few suggestions for those whose pockets are more limited.

In the 'very grand' category:

La Coupole, in the Hôtel Mirabeau (tel: 93 25 45 45), has a discreet charm and plenty of the haute bourgeoisie.

Le Grill de l'Hôtel de Paris, on the 8th floor of the hotel (tel: 93 50 80 80), has sweeping views from Bordighera in Italy to the rock of Monaco opposite, and splendid food and drink. It's hard to know whether this or the Louis XV is better.

Louis XV, in the Hôtel de Paris (tel: 93 50 80 80). Chef Alain Ducasse is so famous that his name is printed in large letters on the hotel awning. With light and pretty period decor, fine silver, painted medallions and ceilings, this is one of the great venues of the Riviera. Expensive, but not in the same league of price and grandeur — suitable perhaps for a birthday or other festive night out:

Le Cygne, 7 ave Princesse Grace (tel: 93 25 59 60) on the ground floor of Houston Palace apartments. Pink table cloths and pastel-shaded murals provide the setting for excellent meals.

Saint Benoit (tel: 93 25 02 34). An interesting restaurant, mainly fish, but rather hard to find. Enter the car park in ave de la Costa just below Le Balmoral, then follow the signs to a concealed staircase leading downwards.

Cheerful and quite a bit cheaper:

Pinocchio, 30 rue Comte Félix Gastaldi (tel: 93 30 96 20). Pizza and pasta. Best reputation among quite a few pizzerias and crêperies up in the old town on le Rocher. This is the cheapest place to eat in Monaco.

Sam's Place, 1 ave Henry Dunant (tel: 93 50 89 33). Over 55yds (50m) up from the Beaumarchais entrance to the Hôtel Hermitage. Low ceilings, lively clientele, with spaghetti, salade niçoise or steak and chips as typical fare.

Among the cafés and bars the **Café de Paris** is the obvious place to take a coffee or aperitif, either indoors or on the agreeable outdoor terrace beside the Casino. Meals are also served here. There are many cafés along the ave Princesse Grace, backing the Larvotto beaches (see also **Accommodation**).

Shopping

In Monaco in general and more particularly in Monte-Carlo there is a dense concentration of the top names in shopping, above all in fashion and jewellery. There are smaller, one-off shops as well, sometimes with slightly lower prices. There are even a few tourist shops selling trivial nick-nacks up in the Old Town. In general, though, it is the top end of the market which is the most interesting and nobody in their right mind would think of Monaco as a place for bargains

The eye-catching entrance to the Café de Paris; refreshment in a stylish setting, by the Casino

or economies. As in Cannes, the
main shopping areas are quite
small and could be explored in
a walk of an hour or so.
The avenue des Beaux-Arts, all
65yds (60m) or so of it,
stretching between the place du
Casino and the square
Beaumarchais, is the epicentre.
On the right hand side going
towards the casino there is a
bank and a perfumery, then
Piaget, selling slightly gaudy
jewellery in a hushed
atmosphere. Next comes
Gianmaria Buccelati, with
jewellery and silverware, each
piece individually designed and
looking not exactly classic but
as if it could have been around
for ages. Next is Adriano
Ribolzi, a very smart antique
shop and 'interior architect',
selling large tapestries and urns
in florid marble. After a flower
shop comes Louis Vuitton with
its characteristic bags, marked
with the distinctive logo, and
finally Cartier with gold watches
and necklaces and little coffee
cups in the window. The other
side of the street, featuring Dior,
Bulgari and Celine, a shop for
smart accessories, is just as
remarkable. Out on the Casino
square there are one or two
others as well, among them Van
Cleef & Arpels.
Near by there are two elaborate
arcades full of boutiques. One,
les Galeries de Metropole, is
underneath the Hôtel Metropole
complex; but this is hard to
visualise since the galleries are
entered from various other spots
and at various levels. They form
a kind of *belle
époque*/post-modern shopping
mall on three storeys with

*Beaulieu's sheltered position drew
many 19th-century visitors, including
the Marquess of Salisbury, British
Prime Minister*

swirling marble staircase,
wrought-iron balconies and
chandeliers. Jean-Claude Jitrois
is there with smart, bright
leatherware and Yves St
Laurent, and shops with names
such as Old Man River.
The other arcade, Les Allées
Lumières, is at the base of the
Park Palace building,
technically 27 ave de la Costa.
Walk up through gardens above
the casino and cross the road to
reach the arcade, which
features women's clothes, smart
and expensive. Jean Jacques
sells Burberrys and Daks and
there is a top-of-the-market
snack bar where one can rest.

WHAT TO SEE ON THE NICE AND MONTE-CARLO COAST

◆◆
BEAULIEU-SUR-MER
Whether you prefer Beaulieu or its seaside neighbour Villefranche (see below) is largely a matter of taste. Beaulieu perhaps has less to recommend it, building for building and street by street. But it has an air of old-fashioned elegance, a fine backdrop of cliff, a crowded harbour, and a reputation for warmth and sheltered gardens. The villa **Kérylos** is an ancient Greek villa as seen through the eyes of archaeologist Theodore Reinach in the early years of this century.

◆◆
CAP FERRAT/ ST-JEAN-CAP-FERRAT
Cap Ferrat, with its solidly luxurious villas set among trees and gardens, offers more to the imagination than to the eye. The cape extends some 2 miles (3km) south of Beaulieu, with an arm off to the east on which the little port and town of St-Jean-Cap-Ferrat is sited. There is a 6-mile (10km) loop of road on the cape but from it you get little more than glimpses of expensive roof below the road and, above, high hedges with gates and intercoms. The well-to-do have at least been able to buy themselves an impenetrable seclusion. But two spots on the cape do offer magnificent views. St-Jean-Cap-Ferrat itself looks back north towards the sheer cliff faces which abound on this stretch of the Riviera; and from

From here, it would be easy to walk down the boulevard des Moulins, the eastward extension of the ave de la Costa. This is a little more like a conventional French shopping street, architecturally rather frumpish, with more interesting shops the further you go. Benetton rubs shoulders, rather surprisingly, with Gucci. One of the most noteworthy establishments is the Pavillon Cristofle, by appointment 'fournisseur' – furnisher – to 'His Serene Highness the Prince of Monaco'. Elaborate see-through glass models of cars, etc.
There are numerous shops in la Condamine, which is the best place for useful things like stationery. Tourist trinkets are sold right on the palace square on le Rocher.

the former home of the Baroness
Ephrussi de Rothschild, now a
museum (well signposted),
there is a fine view down over
the cape from the high saddle at
its centre. St-Jean-Cap-Ferrat is
a pretty place with a lovely
seaside walk around the edges
of its own promontory, the
pointe St-Hospice. The Baroness
Ephrussi de Rothschild built her
large pink palace, with Moorish
touches, mainly to house her
collections of art objects, now
donated to the nation. There are
plenty of them. The dominant
taste is 18th century (guided
tours only). The upper storey
and the gardens – sometimes
looking a little ragged – offer
the finest views.

*Built as a retreat from Saracen raids,
Èze is a cluster of houses on a hill
crowned with a castle*

◆◆◆
THE CORNICHE
Three roads and a railway line
traverse the steep slopes, peaks
and crags of the ruggedly
imposing mountains that lie
along the coast between Nice
and Monte-Carlo. The roads
are, respectively, the **Grande
Corniche** which runs at the
highest level, generally
following the line of the Via
Aurelia, the old Roman road
from Italy to France. The road
along the bottom is the Lower or
Inférieure Corniche and that
between the two is,
unsurprisingly, the **Moyenne**

Corniche. The railway line hugs the coast even more closely than the Inférieure Corniche. The Grande Corniche was built by Napoleon. The Inférieure Corniche was carved out starting in the 18th century and the Moyenne Corniche is a 20th-century invention. Each level has its addicts, but there is no doubt that the majority favours the Moyenne Corniche, arguing that it is high enough to offer fine vistas but close enough to the sea to preserve a sense of Mediterranean excitement. All depends which way you are travelling. If moving east from Nice to Monte-Carlo, then you will be on the exposed, outer side of the road and will see far more. The journey west is perhaps rather disappointing — though, of course, far less terrifying. What is so fine about the Grande Corniche is the soaring sense of height and the breadth of the views. The road first climbs inland out of Nice, offering fine over-the-shoulder views of the city to all but the driver. It rounds the city's observatory to the north with wide views inland, then turns back towards the coast to run out startlingly along a ridge, the Belvedere and Col d'Èze, with views of the hill village of Èze from the Grande Corniche. The road soon passes behind Monte-Carlo through the village of La Turbie before descending, through many twists and turns, to meet the coast at Roquebrune/Cap Martin and terminate in Menton. The Moyenne Corniche has particularly fine views of Villefranche and its roadstead

and is the starting point for the walk up to the pinnacle of Èze. After Monte-Carlo the road becomes less dramatic.

The argument against the Inférieure Corniche is that it can become horribly traffic-clogged in summer so that one's only wish is to escape as far as possible from wheeled vehicles. In its favour is proximity to the sea and the intimate views it offers of Villefranche, Beaulieu and Èze-Bord-de-Mer. Cap-d'Ail is not really visible from the road. To encounter its essence you must plunge steeply down the little one-way system that leads to the waterline. The entry to Monaco, through a packed industrial zone, is ugly beyond expectation.

There are many connecting roads clambering up and down between the various levels of Corniche, enabling the driver to pick and choose, exploit a whim, move up or down as inclination or the traffic situation indicate.

The railway, avoiding traffic, and running along behind beaches and resorts, through tunnels and with views suddenly opening out — as at Villefranche and again in passing Beaulieu — is a perpetual delight; and it is equally good in either direction.

◆◆
ÈZE/ÈZE-BORD-DE-MER

Seen from far off, the village of Èze looks like a wasp's nest, grey and powdery, clinging to its crag 1,200ft (365m) above the sea. The pinnacle or cone that Èze is built on rises from the Moyenne Corniche, 7 ¼ miles

MONACO AND MONTE-CARLO

(12km) from Nice, slightly closer
to Monte-Carlo. This central
position makes it the best
known and most visited of all
the high hill villages of the
region. Èze is certainly worth
the visit, despite the thronging
crowds. Cars and coaches
arrive at the base of the
pinnacle and visitors must then
walk up, entering the tiny but
immaculately restored town by
a handsome 14th-century
gateway. Thereafter come all
the delights of ancient
stonework, combined with
tourist shops and artists' studios
and a pair of spectacularly sited
but small-scale hotels with
restaurants. On the summit of
the crag are the ruins of the
castle, destroyed in 1706. The
castle's remains stand just a little
higher than the spire of the
church rising up from a lower
site on the near-vertical slope.
Somebody has had the genial
idea of creating un jardin
exotique of cactuses among the
ruins of the summit, so simple
and successful an idea it
makes you want to laugh when
you see it.
Èze-Bord-de-Mer is the seaside
dependency of Èze. The railway
runs along behind a busy little
beach and through a small
resort of no great note.

◆◆
MENTON
Menton, often described as a
place of nostalgia and faded
colour, is in fact surprisingly
active and cheerful, with visitors
of all ages. This may be to do
with the recent influx of lively
Italians on the Côte d'Azur; and
if so, this is no bad thing. For it

is certainly the case that the
town's tradition of catering to
invalids and valetudinarians
long ago drifted to a gentle
conclusion, leaving something of
a vacuum.
Backed by mountains and with
its Italianate Old Town rising
steeply above a curving bay,
Menton is not merely one of the
most beautiful places on this
stretch of coast. It also has the
mildest of winter climates. A
British doctor named Benett
pointed this out during the
1850s. His book went into five
editions and was translated into
several languages. The result
was a large number of winter
visitors, particularly British and
German. Hotels grew up along
the front — now called the
promenade du Soleil and
certainly somewhat faded in
appearance, though a very
pleasant place for a stroll. There
was for a time a permanent
English community of 5,000.
Many who came were tubercular
and died young; the graves of
some of them are to be found in
the old cemetery on the hilltop.
William Webb Ellis, inventor of
Rugby football, breathed his last
here. So did the illustrator
Aubrey Beardsley and, later, the
passionate New Zealand short
story writer Katherine Mansfield.
She retreated to a villa in Menton
only to die at the age of 32.
To weigh against all this is the
town's abiding physical beauty,
its returning sense of animation
and a dedication to painting and
music which results in notable
events and interesting
museums. There is also the
golden Menton lemon which
ripens on the trees here all year

round, making Menton a synonym among the French for fertility and warmth.

A visit could well begin with a walk along the **promenade du Soleil** which fronts the new — that is to say, the 19th-century — part of town. The promenade runs along the southern shore and brings one finally to the southern extreme of the bay below old Menton. The **Old Town** faces east, looking along the coast into Italy. There is a harbour here with a quay to either side of it and by walking out along one or other of these one gets a fine view backwards, up into the Old Town, with tall houses rising above one another, a steep jumble surmounted by the large church of **St Michel.** A road runs round the base of the Old Town on a series of arches built by

Menton's position and popularity have made it a combination of Italian and English influences

Napoleon I. He wished to move men and munitions quickly and efficiently without becoming bogged down in the narrow lanes and vertiginous alleys behind.

A double ramp with pebble-mosaic steps and pathway leads up to the church. This is a baroque building with a 16th-century altarpiece and other handsome paintings. In front of the church is a mosaic courtyard with fine views. Immediately above it is the smaller **Chapel of the White Penitents**, another Renaissance building, with an attractively ornamented façade. The steepest exit upwards from this little square now leads towards the old **cemetery.** The cemetery is worth exploring slowly. Most of the English, German and Russian graves are at the lower level, a number of them on a little promontory extending to the south. There are fine views where you can get close enough

to the edge to peep over.
Coming down again from St
Michel, descending by the
ramp but turning right as
opportunity offers, the visitor
will soon reach the eastern end
of a long street that runs back
parallel to the promenade du
Soleil, approximately one block
inland. Different parts of this
street have different names, but
the strolling inhabitants and
holidaymakers, the restaurants
and cafés, small shops and
newspaper stalls make it quite
clear when you have arrived.
This will lead back pleasantly
towards the starting point. Even
so, there will still be a number
of places of interest in Menton
left to visit.

The **Biovès Gardens** in the
town centre are fancifully
bordered with palm and lemon
trees, following the old line
of the river, now long
underground.

The **Jean Cocteau Museum** on
Quai Napoléon III occupies two
small floors of the fortified
bastion, and packs in many fine
works by painter, poet and
film-maker Jean Cocteau. They
include tapestries, a mosaic and
ceramics as well as paintings
and some evocative photos of
Cocteau himself — a must for
any admirer (closed Mondays
and Tuesdays).

There's a good collection of 13th
to 17th-century and 20th-
century paintings in the **Palais
Carolès Museum** (closed
Mondays and Tuesdays), the
former summer residence of
Monaco's Grimaldis. They ruled
over Menton up to 1848, losing
it finally and definitively in 1861.
At the Town Hall on rue de la

République, Cocteau was
invited in 1957 to decorate the
official marriage chamber or
Salle des Mariages (closed
weekends). As at the chapel at
Villefranche, he used a kind of
luminous line-drawing; and
here, as also at Villefranche, one
of the main figures has a fish in
place of an eye.

In January and February, on
successive Sundays, Menton
hosts the attractive Lemon Fair;
and in August, a Chamber
Music Festival is celebrated in
the little square in front of the
church of St Michel, superbly
illuminated.

◆◆
ROQUEBRUNE/CAP MARTIN
Roquebrune's little complex of
castle and medieval village,
well worth the moment or two it
takes to ascend by car from the

*Oranges and lemons, in great
abundance, are one of Menton's
claims to fame, celebrated in
colourful and inventive festivals*

main road, is set just at the Menton end of the Grande Corniche and has become in effect a landward suburb of the village of Cap Martin. Illuminated at night, the **castle** is visible for many miles and is one of the great features of this part of the coast. Roquebrune, the Brown Rock, is itself an extraordinary warren of a place, mounted on a crag which stands clear of a higher cliff rising up behind. The houses are built on top of rocks and into the sides of them, and the little streets and alleys burrow their way about, with all manner of tunnels, arches and covered passageways and steeply rising flights of steps. The castle is France's oldest, originally constructed in the 10th century and a Grimaldi possession from 1350 to 1848. The keep is built of such thick walls that the spaces inside seem laughably small (closed Friday, and mid-November to mid-December). Sir Winston Churchill, the Dutch art forger Hans van Meegeren and le Corbusier, monumental modernist architect, were all associated with Roquebrune. Le Corbusier drowned at Cap Martin in 1965.

Cap Martin is another of the Côte d'Azur peninsulas marked by luxurious villas, high hedges and intercoms at garden gates. Not quite as grand today as Cap Ferrat, it certainly had its moments during the 19th century. Napoleon III's Empress Eugénie wintered here and so did Elizabeth, Empress of Austria. The poet W.B. Yeats died here in 1939.

◆
LA TURBIE
Grande Corniche, above Monte-Carlo.
The Roman road from Italy to Gaul (France, in modern parlance) rose high above the bay of Monaco and crept through a pass behind the Tête de Chien, the mountain bluff that over-shadows it. Here, at 1,575ft (480m) stands the ancient village of La Turbie and a monstrous monument fashioned by the Romans. This was the so-called **Trophée des Alpes** or Alpine Trophy. It stood 165ft (50m) high and 125ft (38m) wide and celebrated the Roman conquest of 44 peoples whom it tactlessly listed. Despite being blown up and generally set upon by locals wishing to build houses, parts of it survived and other parts have been restored. It is a striking if a tasteless object. On the same site, there is also a display of birds of prey. The little stone town around has been smartened up and exudes delicious smells of garlic cookery at lunchtime. Given the difficulties of the terrain, there is a surprising amount of new building in the vicinity. Magnificent views, by night as well as by day.

◆◆
VILLEFRANCHE
This is the first place you meet on rounding Mont Boron, coming out of Nice in an easterly direction, on the lower Corniche. But though scarcely beyond the city boundaries it is a little town of different history and entirely different character from Nice. Its heart is a 17th-century cluster set at the

Villefranche, founded as a free port, is a busy fishing community

base of a bay with waters so deep that they can serve as an anchorage for the largest ships; it looks out across the water to Cap Ferrat – from this distance much like any other headland with houses set among woods and gardens. The total effect of the roadstead, however, is one of almost piercing beauty, seen on the right day and in the right weather. Where once, till France left NATO, US warships lay at anchor, there may now be a sailing ship, perhaps, and a host of yachts and pleasure boats, Cap Ferrat on the far side and on the near side the pleasant garden aspect of the more modern parts of town, rising above old Villefranche. In early days, as its name suggests, Villefranche was a free port. It has steeply stepped streets, with interesting shops and eating places, and frequent glimpses of the water below, always seeming nearer than you

expect. The rue Obscure climbs back from the seafront underneath the houses of the town and is not too pleasant on a wet, cold night. Mostly, though, the weather of Villefranche is exceptionally mild and visitors sit out at restaurants on the little front. There is an impressive **fortress** admired by Vauban, fortress builder extraordinaire. Best of all, though, is the tiny fishing harbour, and the small **chapel of St Peter** just behind it. This was decorated in 1957, by the poet, playwright and artist Jean Cocteau, as a homage to the local fishing community. The effect is beautiful and surprising, light and airy, tender and amusing. Painted scenes of everyday life are interwoven with more formally scriptural subjects but all involve characters who seem as if they could be drawn from the village of Villefranche. It is one of the most delightful works of art on the Riviera, full of surprises.

Restaurants
In Èze, the **Château Eza** (tel: 93 41 12 24) and the **Château de la Chèvre d'Or** (tel: 93 41 12 12) both have small numbers of interesting rooms, elaborate and expensive restaurants and swooping views down to the sea. On the balcony of the Château Eza the following eloquent notice is displayed: 'The management declines any responsibility for items lost over the cliff, which cannot *in any circumstances* be recovered immediately'. **Nid d'Aigle**, a restaurant even closer to the summit (tel: 93 41 19 08) is considerably cheaper.

PEACE AND QUIET:

The Riviera's Wildlife and Countryside

Away from the varied coastline of rugged, inaccessible cliffs and sandy beaches lined with pines, visitors to the Riviera can easily drive into the hills to find slopes covered with a wonderful array of aromatic herbs. Their fragrance perfumes the warm air, while the cool shade of cork oak and chestnut woodlands provides a welcome relief from the midday heat.

Colourful spring flowers often distract the eye from the wealth of insect and bird life to be found in the region. Warblers and nightingales sing from almost every bush while, overhead, noisy parties of bee-eaters hawk for insects, and birds of prey soar on the thermals.

Within easy reach of the Riviera lies the internationally important wetland reserve in the Rhône delta known as the Camargue, which provides a haven for herons, egrets and flamingos. By contrast, a short journey north from the Riviera will take you into the Maritime Alps, with their majestic, snow-capped peaks and hardy plants and animals.

Seas and Coasts

The Riviera is justly famous for its dramatic coastline and blue seas, which lure holidaymakers from far afield and earn the region its name of Côte d'Azur. The Mediterranean is not only beautiful to look at and swim in, but also supports an abundance of marine animals, many of which feature heavily in the cuisine of Provence.

Clary is grown for perfume

Much of the rocky coast is wooded or cloaked in shrubby vegetation, and the cover that this provides supports a variety of nesting birds. Bright yellow serins sing their jingling songs from the topmost branches while warblers prefer to skulk in the shade of the trees. Sardinian warblers are extremely common along the coast and are generally bolder than many of their relatives. The scratchy song often draws the observer's attention to these smart little birds and a close view reveals a prominent red eye-ring.

Because of the weak tides in the Mediterranean, the intertidal zone, such as it is, provides food for comparatively few birds. However, the yellow-legged race of the herring gull is often common and can sometimes be attracted to food. They are occasionally joined by darker-winged lesser black-backed gulls or even slender-billed and Mediterranean gulls. The latter two species are rare in the western Mediterranean and are generally birds of passage along the French coast. Although rock pools are not a

The sea-slug Greilada elegans *is one of many marine animals found along the Riviera coast*

feature of the Riviera coastline, many of the marine animals live close enough to the surface to be seen easily while one is snorkelling. Colourful sea slugs such as *Greilada elegans* crawl gracefully over the surface of the rocks, grazing on minute organisms, while crabs, starfishes and octopuses scurry into crevices.

The Camargue

For anyone interested in wildlife, the regions of the Camargue and la Crau (see below) are well worth a journey to the west of Marseilles. Lying to the south of the town of Arles and between two branches of the River Rhône, the Camargue delta comprises a vast area of marshes and lagoons. These attract huge numbers of breeding and migrant birds, many of which are common nowhere else in Europe. Although the whole region is coming under increasing pressure from farming and tourism, 58 square miles (150 sq km) of the Camargue have been protected since 1928 by nature reserve status. This ensures that at least some of the beaches, sand dunes, saline lagoons and freshwater marshes will be protected for the foreseeable future.

Sandy beaches to the west of the Rhône are the haunt of Kentish plovers. These elegant little waders, with their conspicuous black shoulder patches, run along the shoreline in search of food and nest above the high tide line. Colourful flowers such as sea rocket, sea holly and sea spurge adorn the beaches, and marram grass ensures that the dunes become stabilised. Gulls are often attracted to the shoreline to feed and bathe and are particularly frequent near the mouths of rivers. Slender-billed and Mediterranean gulls are both regular in the Camargue, but are extremely unusual anywhere else in the western Mediterranean.

Hollows between the sand dunes are known as dune 'slacks' and become colonised by stocks and vetches which attract colourful butterflies such as clouded yellows, Queen of Spain fritillaries and the day-flying hummingbird hawk moth. The shelter also encourages nesting birds such as short-toed larks and tawny pipits which build neat little nests among tussocks of grass. The pale, sandy plumage of the tawny pipit allows it to blend in easily with the vegetation and soil, but its presence is frequently given away by its loud, wagtail-like call.

In the more stable areas of dunes, pine woodland develops and provides nesting sites for night and squacco herons and little egrets. The latter were once hunted close to extinction in Europe for their elegant breeding plumes which were valued in the millinery trade.

The Saline Lagoons

Saline lagoons are a widespread and familiar feature of the Camargue. Near the coast the lagoons are extremely saline and are used commercially in salt-extraction, while inland the pools become progressively more brackish as the influence of fresh water is felt.

Saline pools and lagoons are extremely important to the overall ecology of the Camargue and, when conditions are right during the summer months, contain vast numbers of brine shrimps and brine flies. The shrimps in particular are the main source of food for many birds, including the Camargue's most famous inhabitants, the flamingos. Everything about flamingos is

extraordinary. The long legs allow wading in deep water and the long neck is submerged in search of food. The bill is ideally suited for filtering small aquatic animals from the water, and from the diet of shrimps they acquire their most noticeable feature — the pink colour. The Camargue supports several thousand greater flamingos, but although they are common here, it is one of only two sites where they regularly breed in Europe. Even then they do not build their curious mud-platform nests every year

because if feeding conditions
are not exactly right they simply
abandon any attempts.
Although often seen feeding at a
distance, flocks of flamingos in
flight are an inspiring sight.
They often feed in the company
of avocets, black and white
waders which scythe through
the water with their upturned
bills in search of brine shrimps.
This feeding method contrasts
markedly with the stabbing
action of the numerous

*The flamingo, an unmistakable
pink resident of the Camargue*

black-winged stilts, and with the
red-crested pochards, which
dive.
In spring and autumn, tens of
thousands of migrant terns and
waders visit the lagoons of the
Camargue to feed and rest from
their journeys. They often roost
on the embankments and dry
areas of baked mud, sharing
these sites with nesting
stone-curlews, crested and
short-toed larks and pratincoles.
Clumps of scrubby vegetation
have breeding spectacled and
fan-tailed warblers, the latter
continually drawing attention to
themselves with their
'zip-zip-zip' song uttered in
flight. Penduline tits build their
flagon-shaped nests in tamarisk
bushes, while larger trees
accommodate black kites,
golden orioles and lesser grey
shrikes.

Freshwater Marshes
Inland from the Mediterranean,
there are freshwater pools with
a wealth of aquatic vegetation.
Some of these have extensive
reedbeds, and associated
ditches lined with vegetation,
which provide cover and
nesting sites for herons, egrets,
crakes and rails.
A chorus of marsh and edible
frogs sings from the safety of
aquatic vegetation but has great
difficulty competing with the
warblers of the reedbeds in
spring. The song of the great
reed warbler is particularly
frog-like, while that of Savi's
warbler is a long, continuous
reeling sound. Although both
birds generally sing from a
concealed position among the
reeds, they will occasionally

clamber to a high vantage point, allowing the quiet observer a good view.

Montagu's and marsh harriers quarter the reedbeds and take a heavy toll on both warblers and amphibians, especially when they have a hungry brood to feed. Their nests are built among the reeds in the most remote and inaccessible areas of marsh. The frogs are also an important part of the diet of the many herons and egrets which stalk the reedbeds and open water.

Purple herons and little bitterns are both common in the Camargue but are seldom seen except in flight. The best opportunity for a glimpse of these elusive birds is during the breeding season, and especially at dawn and dusk when the birds may fly in and out of the reeds to change over nest duty. In more open, marshy areas little egrets abound and may be

Once persecuted for their elegant plumes, little egrets are common in the Camargue

confused with the similar sized but less frequent squacco heron. These elegant birds have beautiful buff necks and backs, contrasting markedly with their wings, which are conspicuously white in flight.

Crakes and rails are also common in the Camargue, but are more often heard than seen. The incessant whiplash calls of spotted crakes can be heard throughout the night from most reedbeds if you can put up with the mosquitoes. Their chorus is often joined by the monotonous yapping calls of little and Baillon's crakes. Crakes and rails are always shy and retiring birds. However, if you find an open patch of mud in a reedbed which is easy to watch, try sitting quietly near by for an hour or so before dusk, and see what emerges from the cover as the light fades.

La Crau

To the east of the Rhône delta, between the towns of Arles and Port-St-Louis-du-Rhône on the coast, lies a wild and desolate plain known as la Crau. Grazed by a few sheep and goats, which are looked after by the occasional shepherd, the soil is barren and stony. However, its bleak appearance belies the wealth of wildlife it supports, much of which is difficult to find elsewhere in the south of France.

From March to June, la Crau provides a colourful display of aromatic herbs and shrubby plants such as lavender, sage and a variety of species of *Cistus*. These attract butterflies such as spotted and Queen of

A striking male little bustard displaying its neck feathers on the stony plain of la Crau

Spain fritillaries, long tailed blues and skippers. Equally abundant are grasshoppers and bush crickets, many of which fall victim to the grim embrace of the praying mantid.

La Crau is most famous, however, for its birds. The flat landscape gives an open view for wary species like stone-curlew and little bustard. Although the size of small geese, the bustards can be remarkably difficult to see even in open country, since they crouch down at the slightest sign of danger. The best time to see them is perhaps at dawn in the spring when the males perform elaborate courtship displays, in which they puff up their neck feathers, jump in the air with their wings open and emit a loud snorting call. At the height of the display, they often become so absorbed in the ritual that they are less concerned with the presence of man. During the winter, the number of bustards in la Crau is augmented by visitors from northern Europe and flocks of a dozen or more, conspicuous in flight with their black and white wings, are not uncommon. Pin-tailed sandgrouse also favour the semi-desert conditions of the region, often flying considerable distances to find a source of water. Lesser

PEACE AND QUIET

kestrels use wires and bushes as look-outs for small insects and lizards on the ground and even take young larks when just out of the nest. Snakes, and in particular the Montpellier snake, also take a terrible toll on the young of ground-nesting birds. The venom of this back-fanged species acts within seconds on a small bird, and because of their large size, up to 79 inches (2m), the snakes often tackle much larger prey.

Aromatic Plants

French cuisine, widely considered to be among the finest in the world, makes good use of herbs and spices to enhance the flavours of its dishes. Almost all the aromatic plants regularly used in recipes from Provence and the south of France are found growing wild in the region and many are still gathered by hand. A springtime stroll through the countryside of the French Riviera is not only rewarding to the nose, as the plants give off their aromatic

Colourful flowers such as this Provence orchid are a wonderful and familiar feature of spring on the French Riviera

scents, but also to the eye, since most are in flower at this season. As a reminder of your stroll, the scents linger on your clothes for several hours afterwards.

Many of the classic herbs such as marjoram and thyme belong to the mint family, and even rosemary, whose spiky, waxy leaves are popular when cooked with joints of meat, is related. Although superficially similar in appearance to mint, basil, with its whorls of purple flowers, gives off a wonderful aroma when crushed and is a real favourite in southern French cooking, being used fresh in salads and sauces.

The umbellifer or carrot family also contains many plants which are popular in French cooking. Chervil is used as a fresh garnish, as are the leaves of dill, and the seeds and flower heads of the latter are used to flavour pickles. Fennel, with its feathery leaves, is used both for its aniseed flavour and as a tasty bulb vegetable. However, the most famous ingredient of French cooking, namely garlic, is a member of neither the mint nor the carrot families, but is actually a member of the lily family.

Aromatic plants are also used in the perfume industry, an extremely important factor in the economy of the south of France. Plants such as clary and lavender are of such importance that they are sometimes grown commercially and colourful fields are a familiar sight. Many of the plants end up in the town of Grasse, the perfume centre of the French Riviera, which is also famous for its crystallised fruit

and flowers (see also page 46). Here, the leaves and flowers of the aromatic plants are distilled to produce scented oils, a process which can be viewed in most of the town's factories.

Hills and Mountains

Inland from the dramatic coastline of the French Riviera the land rises to undulating ranges of hills and mountains. Many of the hills are still cloaked in Mediterranean woodland comprising cork and holm oaks, pines and chestnuts, but much of the area is now cleared and covered instead with aromatic shrubs and herbs. To the east and north of the perfume town of Grasse, in Haut Provence, lies a series of impressive mountains with dramatic gorges cut by tiny rivers. However, these rifts in the Pre-Alps of Grasse lack the grandeur of the magnificent Verdon canyon further east which is 12 miles (20km) long and, in places, several hundred feet deep.

During the summer, rock buntings and rock thrushes haunt the slopes of the gorges, while alpine swifts circle overhead, feeding on insects carried in the updraughts. In the winter, the gorges sometimes play host to birds from the Alps which descend to lower altitudes to escape the harsh conditions. Most elegant of these visitors is the aptly-named wallcreeper, which searches the rock faces for insects, particularly in the vicinity of waterfalls and on damp cliffs. Between Toulon and Cannes lie the impressive Esterel and

Maures massifs. Although often ravaged by forest fires, some areas are still covered in woodland and the Dom state forest inland from Le Lavandou in the Maures massif is easily accessible. The forest floor is adorned with colourful lilies, irises, tree heathers and orchids, including the delightful Provence orchid, *Orchis provincalis*. The cork oaks and pines provide nesting sites for booted and short-toed eagles, which often soar overhead on thermals.

If large birds of prey unwittingly stray into the territory of a pair of ravens these largest members of the crow family lose no time in mobbing the intruder. In fact, listening for their loud cronking alarm calls is often a good way to find birds of prey. The same wild, hilly terrain is also shared by choughs, red-billed relatives of the raven. Their far-carrying 'chough' call and wing feathers, forming distinct fingers, make them easy to identify.

The Mercantour National Park

Lying along the Italian border, the Mercantour National Park protects 173,000 acres of some of the most dramatic and imposing scenery in the Maritime Alps. The reserve, which lies between 4,900ft (1,500m) and 9,800ft (3,000m) above sea level, adjoins the Valdieri-Entracque reserve in Italy and has good populations of alpine birds, mammals and plants.

The resort of Le Boreon, north of St Martin-Vesubie, is a good place from which to explore the national park. The lower slopes are wooded with pines and larch but the trees soon give way to colourful alpine meadows and boulder-strewn slopes and finally to permanent snow. Around the edge of the tree line, citril finches and ortolan and rock buntings nest and feed, while chamois graze every accessible piece of succulent vegetation.

Alpine meadows support a wealth of orchids, gentians and bellflowers and are home to one of the Alps' most endearing mammals. The guinea pig-sized Alpine marmot excavates burrows and often forms loose colonies. Where left undisturbed it can become quite indifferent to the presence of man. If a marmot spots a griffon vulture or a golden eagle, however, it is a different matter and it loses no time in alerting its neighbours with a shrill call.

As the snow line retreats up the mountain sides in the spring and summer, scree slopes and lichen-covered boulders are revealed. These provide an ideal habitat for another curious inhabitant of the Alps, the ptarmigan, a grouse-sized gamebird which shows remarkable adaptation to its harsh and changing environment. During the summer months its plumage is mottled to blend in with the broken terrain. This camouflage would be completely useless, however, in the winter when snow blankets the ground, so, after its autumn moult, the ptarmigan acquires a pure white plumage.

Alpine marmots haunt the meadows of the Maritime Alps

The mountain hare also adopts the strategy of changing its coat to suit the season. During the summer its blue-grey fur is a perfect match for the lichens and mosses, while in winter it turns pure white to match the ice and snow. The only things left unchanged are the tips of its ears, which are always black.

Woodland

Were it not for extensive clearance over the centuries, much of the French Riviera would still be covered by woodland, the 'natural' vegetation of the region. Today the French have an active forestry department which controls and prevents unnecessary damage to the remaining woodlands; but regrettably they can do little to combat the extensive and often deliberately started forest fires that are an almost annual feature of the dry summers.

Many of the trees are evergreen; by retaining their leaves throughout the year, they can grow during the cool, wet winters, and the thick, waxy coating helps resist desiccation during the summer.

Along the sandy shores, the aptly named umbrella or stone pine, with its flattened canopy, is common. Its dense canopy casts a deep shade, allowing little else to grow underneath, and its fallen needles often form a neat carpet. Umbrella pines produce large cones whose seeds are often used in cooking. Inland, cork oaks are common and provide a valuable harvest of cork evey 10 years or so. They often grow alongside maritime pines, since neither species grows well on limestone.

Limestone soils, by contrast, have woodlands composed of aleppo pines with twisted trunks and a more open canopy. The ground vegetation is generally richer than under maritime pines and, especially in clearings, thyme, rue, rosemary, *Cistus* and many species of orchid can be found. Particularly striking are the members of the bee orchid family, such as the early spider orchid, with its rounded, downy flowers, and the imposing violet limodore. The latter species is elegant enough to stand comparison with many exotic, cultivated orchids. Butterflies such as the green hairstreak and scarce swallowtail pay frequent, nectar-gathering visits to the flowers along with chafers and bees.

Although resident mammals such as red squirrel and pine marten are shy and have abandoned woodland close to habitation, they are still found in more remote areas. However, firecrests and serins are found in almost every pine wood, and twisted and split trunks of cork and holm oak provide nesting holes for hoopoe and Scop's and little owls.

Open Country
Over the centuries, most of the lowlands and hills of the Riviera have been gradually cleared by man of their natural woodland. Agriculture now occupies much of the open country, but in places more natural vegetation has developed. When lime-free soils are cleared of maritime pines the land acquires a shrubby type of habitat known as *maquis,* whereas when aleppo pine woods are cleared on limestone, a more open,

The Riviera's abundant insect life provides ideal feeding conditions for long-eared and other species of bat

barren-looking habitat known as *garigue* develops.

Vineyards and olive groves provide perches and nesting sites for red-backed, woodchat and lesser grey shrikes. These keen-eyed predators are always on the look-out for insects and lizards, which comprise the majority of their diet. Larger victims are often impaled on a thorn and then subsequently dismembered. Bee-eaters float overhead uttering their liquid calls and catching dragonflies and bees on the wing, their plumage seemingly containing every colour in the rainbow.

Maquis vegetation is especially colourful in the spring. Strawberry tree, lentisc and tree heathers predominate and harbour a variety of breeding birds such as Sardinian and subalpine warblers and blackcaps, while an understorey of rock-roses, honeysuckles and the spiny, broom-like *Calycotome spinosa* attract a multitude of insects.

For the first three months of the year, much of the *garigue* of the Riviera becomes a riot of golden yellow with the flowers of the gorse *Ulex parviflorus* interspersed with the spiny-leaved kermes oak. This is followed by a succession of colourful species such as orchids, vetches and clovers, including the starry clover, whose sepals spread in fruit to resemble a miniature star. Insects and spiders scurry along the ground and many fall victim to the predatory larvae of ant-lions. Some species live in specially dug holes in the ground, into which the prey fall,

In contrast to their rather gruesome larvae, adult ant-lions have elegant markings

while others are free-roving and catch their victims with their ferocious mandibles. In contrast to the rather grotesque larvae, the adults are elegant, and *Palpares libelluloides* (it has no common name) in particular has beautiful blotched wings and an orange abdomen.

Bats

The hot summers and mild winters of the Riviera are ideal for insects, which provide an almost endless supply of food for bats. Night-flying beetles, bugs and especially moths support up to 18 species of bat which are regularly found in the south of France.

Long-eared bats prefer to feed around the leaf canopy of trees and roost during the day in hollow trunks and branches. Other species, such as pipistrelle and Daubenton's, catch moths and mosquitoes over rivers and ponds, and roost in rock crevices. During the winter, caves provide an ideal environment, with stable temperatures and shelter from the elements.

SHOPPING

SHOPPING

There is no doubt that shops and shopping are a source of great interest on the French Riviera — indeed, one of the focal points for visitors. It is above all the range which makes the shopping so fascinating — everything from the most chic and expensive in the world to the comfortable and familiar and even the plain shabby. There is also a strong local emphasis, with plenty of products from the area and a profusion of colourful open air markets. To start at the top: in terms of fashion, jewellery and all manner of accessories, Cannes and Monte-Carlo are quite simply the smartest places in

Shops in Antibes, as in other Riviera towns, range from tourist trinkets to high style

France outside Paris. The difference between them and Paris is one of quantity rather than quality. The leading shopping areas of Cannes and Monte-Carlo are small enough for one good walk to give the shopper or browser an overall picture. All the great names are there in an array of solid luxury and highest style. Nice, too, has its smart shops but here the range is wider, with the full panoply of a substantial city. St Tropez, on the other hand, is out on the wild side, with plenty of high fashion in the most extravagant designs. Details on shopping in each of these places are given in their individual entries.

Then there are the local products. The Côte d'Azur produces magnificent olive oil (and many interesting objects made of olive wood). Candied fruit is a speciality. There are very pretty – and instantly recognisable – printed cotton fabrics from Provence. There is good local glass and plenty of attractive pottery. All these can, of course, be bought in a city like Nice, but individual towns have their specialities (Biot, for example, in glassware) and this is mentioned as appropriate under individual entries.

Finally, there are the markets, many held outdoors. St Tropez is a good example, with a wonderful range of goods twice weekly at its venue in the place des Lices. One stall may be selling olives prepared in up to 20 different ways. Another has second-hand clothing; another again is selling little 19th-century paintings. Fruit and vegetables are bright and various and look tantalisingly fresh. The pizza man is there as well, with a roaring pizza oven built into his mobile shop. Local inhabitants wander in and out with vegetable baskets and long loaves of bread tucked under their arms, a living theatre in which it is easy and delightful to take part.

FOOD AND DRINK
Eating on the Riviera
Given the large number of tourists, there is an infinite variety of eating places, with plenty of hamburgers in evidence as well as grand establishments serving the finest French food. Restaurants display their menus outside so you can see in advance what you are getting into. The *prix fixe* or set price menus are generally the best value.

Much of the food, and generally the most interesting, is in fact local in character. The two key words are *Provençal* and *Niçois*. The cuisine of the whole region is dominated by that wonderful southern mix of olive oil, onion and fresh tomatoes, black olives, anchovies and garlic and all the fish and meat dishes in which one or several of these ingredients may be used as a basis. The strong, aromatic herbs of the deep south also figure large. Nice itself is a fine and distinctive culinary centre, regarded as having its own cuisine. It uses the same materials as the rest of the coast but in so individual a way that sometimes they bear the name of the city. *Salade niçoise* is the most famous example but often on menus you will come across other items described as *Niçois*. They are generally worth a try.

Salads and Vegetables
When one thinks about the cooking of southern France, it is usually vegetables which come to mind first, both because they are delicious and locally produced and because it is vegetables in the broadest sense which establish the essential tastes. A dish described as *à la provençale* will involve an olive oil based sauce of onion and tomato, often

FOOD AND DRINK

with thyme or other herbs, rendered down to its essence by slow cooking. Sometimes, it has to be said, the cooking is hasty and one has the impression that a dish has been swamped.

Salads play a large part all along the coast, with *salade niçoise* — always served as a starter — occupying a prominent position. There are many varieties of this but authorities agree that it must at least include quartered hard-boiled eggs, tomatoes, black olives and anchovy fillets, with garlic in the dressing. Tuna

Perfume and cookery are two Riviera specialities which are often combined in aromatic dishes

fish and lettuce are also fairly standard components. *Mesclun* is a salad of lettuce and dandelion. Another common starter is *crudités* — a dish made up quite simply of sliced raw vegetables with a mayonnaise dip. Locally produced artichokes and asparagus are much favoured along the Côte d'Azur. Ratatouille, an olive oil based stew of aubergines and tomatoes, is both common and much valued. It is perhaps the most famous and most southern in feeling of all vegetable dishes.

Soups

Soups are a great tradition here. The best known is probably *pistou*, based on the pounded-up mixture of olive oil, basil and pine-nuts which the Italians call *pesto*. But while the Italians use it as a pasta sauce, in Nice in particular, it is used as a flavouring for soups with many vegetables. Fish soups, discussed below, are, if possible, even more delicious.

Fish

It is no surprise that fish is central to eating habits along the south coast of France. The sea bass or *loup de mer* is particularly prized, excellent when grilled. The red mullet (*rouget*) and John Dorey (*daurade*) are also popular. But it is fish mixtures — stews and soups — which seem most characteristic of the area. Marseilles, along the coast, is the home of *bouillabaisse*, a saffron-tinted fish stew containing many varieties and surrounded with much

Fresh seafood is a staple menu item at the Coco Beach Restaurant in Nice, where a high reputation is matched by high prices

mystique. It is offered in numerous restaurants on the Riviera but it is extremely expensive and should generally be ordered in advance. *Bourride* is a slightly simpler fish stew, made with white fish and garlic and also common on menus. The more humble-sounding fish soup, however, is often surprisingly elaborate and may give quite as much satisfaction. It is generally based on rockfish, strong in flavour but tiresomely boney when grilled, with a good quantity of shell-fish to go with

them. It is served with grated cheese, little hard morsels of toast and a mayonnaisy sauce called *rouille* which you decant into your soup. Be warned, though – this can be fiery with chilli and should be tasted first. *Aïoli* is a fierce mayonnaise full of crushed garlic and most often served with fish.

Meat Dishes
The mountainsides of southern France harbour many flocks of sheep, and lamb naturally figures large, often grilled and tangy with herbs. Lamb may also be served *à la provençale*. Beef is often braised with vegetables and garlic to create the tasty brew described on menus as *daube de boeuf*.

Boeuf niçois is much the same, with the addition of black olives.

Pasta and Pizza

The closer to Italy, the more Italian the style. Some say the pizzas get better all along the coast from St Tropez to Menton. Freshly made pasta of all kinds is one of the great treats of Nice.

Other Specialities

Anchoiade is a little anchovy tart served as a starter, and the *pissaladière* is an onion tart with black olives – both delicious. *Pan bagnat*, often served at sandwich stalls, is a bap of doughy bread the size of a Frenchman's beret with a filling similar to *salade niçoise*. *Socca*, a great favourite in Nice, is a pancake of ground chickpeas, sometimes made in spectacularly large frying pans.

Drink

Beer, wine, spirits and champagne all flow freely, but at a price, on the Riviera. There are beers and spirits of all kinds, French and imported, and, naturally enough, all the wines and champagnes of France. As regards local wines, there is little activity at the eastern, Italian end of the Riviera, though Nice itself does produce small quantities. From Fréjus and St Raphael onwards, going west, vineyards are a common sight. Sometimes they are surprisingly high up, particularly in valleys in the Maures massif. These vineyards mark the start of the Côtes de Provence region. Reds and whites are both produced, but locals set more store by their own rosé. It is well worth

acquiring the taste for this wine; Côtes de Provence rosés can give great satisfaction, especially in the heat of summer.

The south of France is a wonderful place for taking refreshment – whether coffee, soft drink or alcoholic – in any of the multitudinous cafés that crowd squares and pavements and throng behind the beaches. One aperitif very commonly enjoyed by the French is *pastis*, an aniseed liquor that turns cloudy when water is added. A chink of ice completes the pleasure.

ACCOMMODATION

A good deal of the high style of the 19th century still lives on; and in all the main resorts except St Tropez (which had none) some, at least, of the grand hotels of early days survive, often splendidly restored and chock-a-block with period flavour. There are also top class modern hotels. Yet somehow, despite its reputation for wealth and luxury, the Côte d'Azur caters for all income brackets. There is often bargain accommodation to be had in town centres, particularly in Nice, and there is generally cheap accommodation behind the coast, well within day-tripping distance. This means that younger people, families with children and those on economy budgets can enjoy the pleasures of a far more rural southern France and still have access to the sea.

Hotels fall into one of five grades – from one-star up to

One of the Riviera's private, one-
to three-star hotels known as
Logis de France: Auberge Belles
Terrasses at Tourrettes-sur-Loup

four-star and finally four-star
luxury. The quantity of stars in
relation to the number of rooms
gives a good indication of
comparative prices. A glance at
any hotel list will quickly reveal,
for instance, that four beds out
of five in Monaco are in four-star
luxury hotels; the majority in
neighbouring Menton are two-
and three-star. The conclusion is
that Menton will be much
cheaper not just in terms of
hotels but across the whole
range of facilities. If economy is
a consideration, stay there and
day-trip to Monaco and
Monte-Carlo. But the
experience of the great hotels is
so extraordinary that there is a
strong case for economising for
most of a holiday and then
splashing out, no expense
spared, for a final night or two at
one of the great ones – the
Négresco in Nice, say; the
Carlton or the Majestic in
Cannes; the Hôtel de Paris or
the Hermitage in Monte-Carlo
(for hotel booking, see **Tourist**
Offices; information also
available from French
Government Tourist Office).
Breakfast is often an extra and
can be expensive; cafés can
make a pleasant alternative. In
your room, don't be surprised if
a neck-wrenching bolster is
lying across the top of the bed

— hotels have pillows too and will readily supply them. Often, there is a clutch of pillows concealed in the wardrobe. Water in hotel bathrooms is safe to drink. Dreadful plumbing is mostly a thing of the past, though Nice in particular has some cheap hotels which have not yet been knocked into shape.

Self-catering holidays are readily available in the south of France. Details from the French Government Tourist Office, 178 Piccadilly, London W1V 0AL. Camping and youth hostels are other possibilities: see **Camping** and **Student and Youth Travel** in the Directory, below.

WEATHER AND WHEN TO GO

The Côte d'Azur follows the old geography lesson precept about the Mediterranean: hot dry summers, warm wet winters — except that the winters can also be chilly at night and in the early morning. The middle of the day is often clear and brilliant. The rain, when it comes, generally goes away again quite soon. But it can rain buckets, seemingly all at once. Then there is the wind. In summer, the breezes are often gentle and cooling but there is a variety of fiercer winds as well. The most famous is the *mistral*, which comes tearing down from the north out of a clear sky and generally blows for several days at a time. Some places are sheltered; others catch the full force of it. Winds are discussed in the south of France with a tone of affectionate exasperation. Summer clothes should be light, though the fashion-conscious will wish to bring a varied wardrobe. In winter, the best plan is to dress in thin layers, allowing for the removal of clothes as the day heats up and then for putting them on again towards the evening.

NIGHTLIFE AND ENTERTAINMENT

Nightlife on the Riviera is intense and pacy and, in some resorts, decidedly noisy, too. The Beautiful People party the night away and often have difficulty dragging themselves to the beach by lunchtime. There are discos and nightclubs ranging from the very smartest in Monte-Carlo and Cannes to the comparatively raucous in Juan-les-Pins. The Riviera is also well equipped with casinos: not just the big one in Monte-Carlo, but others all along the coast — Nice, Cannes, St Raphael, etc. Night-time entertainment is a major part of life on the Riviera. Culture also looms large. Those

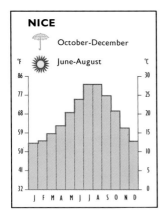

NICE

October-December

°F   June-August   °C

Street entertainment, Provençal style: a relaxing game of pétanque, which involves rolling steel bowls towards a marker

interested in 20th-century art will already know that the Côte d'Azur possesses what must be among the finest collections of paintings and sculpture outside Paris and New York. Such giants as Matisse and Picasso lived here and the area is rich in their work. Events such as the Cannes Film Festival and the Jazz Festival in Nice are major international attractions. In addition, there are in season literally scores of top class performances in all the arts, whether popular or esoteric. Ballet, classical music, rock music, etc are all so massively represented that sometimes it becomes almost impossible to choose which to go to.

HOW TO BE A LOCAL

There are no amazing mysteries about how to behave in France. It is one of the most civilised of nations and appreciates good manners, comprehensible in any language. This is not to say the French cannot be rude; they can, and it is clear that people serving tourists do get tired and fed up. But courtesy and friendliness are far more common and, often, like behaviour will be met with like. In conversation it is polite to address those you are talking to

as *monsieur* or *madame* without
necessarily using the surname
– as in *bonjour, madame* or
bonsoir, monsieur. The attention
of waiters is still attracted by the
rather old-fashioned sounding
garçon – best called out,
however, in a friendly tone.
Nice in particular, is an
emotional, not to say
hot-blooded, place, with hugs,
kisses and quarrels all on lavish
Latin display. Liveliness of
temperament is the rule among
local people along the coast;
there always seems to be plenty
of laughter in the south.
Topless bathing is acceptable
almost everywhere, though it is
far less common on large town
beaches, as in Nice. It conveys
no sexual message whatsoever.
Nude bathing is common but
generally restricted to easily
recognisable areas.
Attitudes to dress off the beach
can be surprisingly stiff.
Multi-lingual signs displayed at
key points in Monaco read as
follows:
'Apart from the immediate
vicinity of the beaches and
bathing facilities it is forbidden
to walk around
– bare-chested
– wearing only a swimming
   costume
– barefoot.
Failure to comply with these
regulations could result in
prosecution.'

CHILDREN

The French Riviera is not the
world's best place for children.
It is sophisticated and crowded
and this applies to beaches as
much as to dry land. Journeys

by car with children in summer
are horrible – for children and
grown-ups too. This being said,
there are, in addition to the sea
itself, a number of attractions:
Marineland, near Antibes: daily
displays by dolphins, seals,
penguins, etc; shaded
restaurant. Just off N7, 2 miles
(3km) from Antibes, 7½ miles
(12km) from Nice.
Water park, near Fréjus: ideal
for all the family (see **Fréjus**
entry). Also a zoo/safari park.
Just south of Fréjus plage on the
coast road.
Oceanographic Institute,
Monaco: a fine aquarium and
many other displays (see
Monaco entry). Monaco also has
the National Museum, a
collection of dolls in an
engaging villa in the ave
Princesse Grace.
Zygofolis amusement park, rte
de Digne, near Nice. Family fun.
For teenagers there is roller
skating and skate boarding all
over the Riviera, as well as
water-skiing, cycling, etc – and
watching the extraordinary
ways of Riviera adults.

TIGHT BUDGET

For tips on where and how to
stay, see **Accommodation,**
above. For snacks and cheaper
eating, see **Food and Drink.** It is
possible to get by on a relatively
small amount of money on the
Côte d'Azur, particularly by
staying inland and day-tripping
to the coast. The coast presents
marvellous opportunities to see
how the other tenth lives and for
some, no doubt, to daydream.
But, even so, it is more fun when
you are feeling flush.

DIRECTORY

Arriving

Entry formalities Only a passport is required for nationals of European countries (except Turkey); visas for all others. Check, though, with a travel agent or the French Government Tourist Office (for addresses see **Tourist Offices**, below), since visa policy is subject to review.

By air Most travellers arrive by air at Nice-Côte d'Azur airport, 4 miles (7km) southwest of the city. The run-in is exhilarating in daylight, with views of the coast and mountains for a few minutes before the plane comes in, apparently about to land on water, in practice landing on a patch of artificial ground

Flowers and tropical plants flourish in Menton's warm climate

pushing out into the sea. The airport terminal is fairly small but efficient, handling several million passengers each year. There are bank and change facilities; car hire (see below); post office; restaurant and snack bar; souvenir and fashion accessory shops in the main departure lobby; duty free, past customs on departure.

Transport from airport Taxis are very expensive. There is a half-hourly bus to central Nice; also a bus westwards to Antibes, Juan-les-Pins and Cannes. There is a convenient railway service (see below) right along the coast from Menton to St Raphael and Fréjus, though not St Tropez, which can be picked up in any town centre. Heli-air Monaco flies direct from the airport to the principality (lands in Fontvieille), flight time about

8 minutes. Desk near exit from customs.

By road From Paris, south by Autoroute (toll-paying motorway). But beware particularly weekends at the end of July and during August, when heavy holiday traffic makes the non-motorway network infinitely more agreeable.

By rail This is an excellent way of reaching the Côte d'Azur. A fast, efficient and pleasant service is offered by French National Railways (Société Nationale des Chemins de Fer Français, SNCF); details from travel agents. Best to take high speed train TGV ('train à grande vitesse') for daylight journeys (advance booking required); sleeper by night. The journey can also be made on various forms of reduced-fare rail-pass which then enable you to use the train as the main means of to-ing and fro-ing on the Riviera. There is a useful combined air-rail option with flights to Paris, easy transfer and on to final destination by rail.

For motorists, there is an efficient year-round motorail service from Calais to Nice. In summer, from Boulogne, Calais and Dieppe to Avignon, St Raphael, Nice. Highly recommended, especially for those wishing to avoid the long haul south during the French holiday season (see also **Customs Regulations**).

Camping

Camping and caravanning are both popular. Campsites on the Côte d'Azur are plentiful but are often full in July and August, making pre-booking essential. French tourist offices have leaflets on camping in France generally. Send stamps with your request. There is also a *Michelin* guide on camping. Campsites are officially graded from one- to four-star depending on the amenities offered, which may include 24-hour security, shops and restaurants, and elaborate sports facilities.

Car Breakdown

Put on hazard lights and place warning triangle 55yds (50m) behind the car. On autoroute, ring from emergency phones located every mile (2km) to contact breakdown service; fixed fee marked on phone booth. Off motorway, police will advise on local emergency services.

Car Hire

Many package holidays include car hire as an option. Highly recommended for travellers who want to get into the Riviera hinterland with its hill villages and mountainous landscape. All the main car hire companies have desks at Nice-Côte d'Azur airport. Some telephone numbers there: Avis: 93 21 36 33; Hertz: 93 21 36 72; Europcar: 93 21 36 44. There are generally plenty of cars available, sometimes with special offers in winter. Difficulties may be experienced, though, at times of particular events such as the Cannes Film Festival or the Monte-Carlo Grand Prix. Cars may also be hired in other towns.

Shops come in all shapes and sizes: a Nice street vendor

Chauffeur Driven Cars
These can be organised via car hire companies and are very expensive.

Chemist
see **Pharmacist**

Crime
Displays of wealth, which are plentiful on the Riviera, are naturally attractive to thieves. Expensive cars are most at risk and drivers will be well advised not to pull in at night on unmanned motorway rest areas. In crowded places, beware pickpockets.

Customs Regulations
Travellers arriving from EEC countries may import duty free into France and export duty free into their own countries (for their use only) if purchased in normal shops, tax paid:
300 cigarettes or 150 cigarillos; 75 cigars or 15 ounces (400g) of tobacco; 1.5 litres of alcohol over 22 per cent vol (or 38.8 deg. proof) or 3 litres not over 22 per cent vol or fortified sparkling wine, plus 5 litres still table wine; 75g of perfume and 375 cl of toilet water; 2lbs (1kg) of coffee or ⅟₂ lb (200g) of tea (or 15 ounces (400g) of instant coffee or tea, or 3 ounces (80g) of essence);
if purchased in duty free shops: 200 cigarettes or 100 cigarillos; 50 cigars or 9 ounces (250g) of tobacco; 1 litre of alcohol over 22 per cent vol (or 38.8 deg. proof) or 2 litres not over 22 per cent vol or fortified sparkling wine, plus 2 litres still table wine; 50g of perfume and 250cl of toilet water; 2lbs (1kg) of coffee or ⅟₂ lb (200g) of tea (or 15 ounces (400g) of instant coffee or tea, or 3 ounces (80g) of essence).
No alcohol for under 17's.
In addition, travellers may export without duty goods up to value of Ff2,400 (Ff620 for those under 15), including 4⅟₂lbs (2kg) fruit or vegetables (except potatoes), five plants or parts of plants (not chrysanthemums or

trees), a small bunch of cut flowers, 2lbs (1kg) of fresh meat and 2lbs (1kg) cooked meat (not pork, poultry or offal) and 50 litres of beer. For regulations on money at entry and exit, see **Money Matters.**

Traditional costume is worn in Nice during festivals and events

Domestic Travel

Air Air Inter is the French internal airline, linking more than 50 cities, among them Marseilles and Toulon as well as Nice. Information via Air France and travel agents. Some private airlines also serve smaller towns.

Bus Regular services, though not very frequent, cover the Côte d'Azur and its hinterland. For most places behind the coast, the only alternative is a hire car or organised coach trip. Main towns have bus stations (*gares routières*), with timetable information available. There is no train to St Tropez and those using public transport along the Riviera will be obliged to take the bus. Regular departures from the little square immediately behind St Raphael railway station. Slow and tedious in summer, not bad in winter.

Rail See **Arriving,** above for journey to Côte d'Azur. Details of French National Railways (Société Nationale des Chemins de Fer Français, SNCF) from travel agents.

One of the features of the Riviera is the railway line which runs behind the coast from Fréjus/St Raphael to Menton. One or two stretches of the line are fairly routine but parts are good to spectacular, particularly rounding the Esterel massif and running along the bottom of the

Nice-Monaco Corniche. Has to be one of the livelier railway journeys of the world. Also, in summer, the best way to move along the coast without getting caught in traffic jams. There are numerous passes, reductions and special deals which may suit your own requirements. Rail information: Nice (tel: 93 87 50 50); Monaco (tel: 93 30 25 53).

Taxis Very expensive and not allowed to cruise. They must pick up at ranks (*stations de taxi*) found at airports, railway stations and elsewhere. Some telephone numbers: Cannes railway station: 93 38 30 79; Nice: 93 82 32 32; St Tropez: 94 97 40 86. Always check that there is a meter and consult in advance with driver if journey takes you out of town.

Ferries Car and passenger services from Nice, Toulon and Marseilles to a variety of ports in Corsica, journey time 5 to 10 hours depending on destination. Operator is SNCM, Société Nationale Corse-Méditerranée (Nice branch: tel: 93 89 89 89).

Cars

Accidents: ask witnesses to stay in order to make statements, and contact the police. Exchange insurance details with other drivers involved.

Documents required: valid driver's licence, not provisional − minimum driving age is 18 (international licence not required for visitors from US, UK or Western Europe); the vehicle's registration document, plus a letter of authorisation from the owner if not accompanying the vehicle; current insurance certificate (green card not mandatory but remains internationally recognised and can be helpful). Also, a nationality plate or sticker is required.

Entry formalities: no restrictions on taking vehicles into France provided this is for no longer than six months in any period of 12 months.

Driving in France: keep to the right (*serrez à droite*), and all will be logical and straightforward − with one major difference. Though main roads have priority (*passage protégée*), right of way is otherwise given to vehicles coming in from the right. Increasingly, traffic already on roundabouts has priority over vehicles entering, as indicated on roadsigns.

Driving on the Riviera: heavy traffic means that the experience can be slow and exasperating in summer, with plenty of horn-blowing and free-flowing emotion; the coast road is the slowest. The autoroute running behind − A8 − is fast and convenient and in places dramatic. Winter driving is more fun, though beware of ice on sheltered stretches of mountain roads and of snow inland.

Insurance: fully comprehensive cover is advisable.

Petrol: service stations are numerous. Unleaded petrol is available (list of service stations offering unleaded petrol is obtainable from French Tourist Offices).

Speed limits: autoroutes/ toll-motorways: 130 kph (81 mph), dry weather; 110 (68 mph) in rain or limited visibility. Dual

DIRECTORY

carriage-ways and non-toll
motorways: 110 kph (68 mph)
good weather, 100 (65 mph) bad.
Other roads, 90 kph (55 mph)
good weather, 80 (50 mph) bad.
In towns 60 kph (37 mph).
Restricted area starts at town
sign, ends at town exit sign
marked with a bar through the
name.

Driving
(see **Domestic Travel** – cars)

Electricity
220 volt (50 cycles AC) is now
the norm, with standard
continental two pin round plug,
making an adaptor essential for
British or American appliances.
Some country districts are said
still to be 110V, but they are
hard to find.

Embassies and Consulates
British Embassy: 35 rue du
Faubourg St Honoré, 75383 Paris
Cedex 08 (tel: (1) 42 66 91 42).
US Embassy: 2 rue Saint-
Florentin, 74042 Paris Cedex 01
(tel: (1) 42 61 80 75/42 96 14 88).
Canadian Embassy: 35 ave
Montaigne, 75008 Paris (tel: (1)
47 23 01 01).
Consulates on south coast:
British: 11 rue Paradis, 06000
Nice (tel: 93 82 32 04); 24 ave du
Prado, 13006 Marseilles (tel: 91
53 43 32/91 37 66 95).
US: 31 rue Maréchal Joffre,
06000 Nice (tel: 93 88 89 55).
Canada: 24 ave du Prado, 13006
Marseilles (tel: 91 37 19 37).

Emergency Telephone Numbers
Police: 17
Fire: 18 (*sapeurs pompiers*)
Ambulance: 18
Ambulance service Monaco: 93
30 04 85

24-hour emergency doctors
Antibes: 93 61 09 09
Cannes: 93 38 10 11/93 38 39 38
Nice: 93 83 01 01

Entertainment Information
Many Côte d'Azur towns have
their own *Offices de Tourisme*
or *Sydicats d'Initiative* (see
Tourist Offices, below). These
generally have leaflets on
entertainments. Newspapers list
entertainments and carry
relevant advertisements –
notably *Nice-Matin* at the
eastern end of the Riviera
(including Monaco) and
Var-Matin in the west; and the
weekly *Semaine des
Spectacles.* Hotel desks are
generally well-informed.

Entry Formalities
see **Arriving**

Guidebooks
There are many good guide-
books to France in general and
a number concerned exclusively
with the south of France/Côte
d'Azur/ Riviera. One or two
general guides:
Blue Guide France, A & C Black
(1988).
Concentrates on art, history,
architecture.
Guide to France, AA/Hachette
(1988).
Print rather small but volume of
information is huge and sensibly
chosen.
The Rough Guide to France by
Baillie, Salmon and Sanger, pub.
Routledge and Kegan Paul
(1988).
Another in this practical and
illuminating series, mostly used
by low budget travellers but
very often packed with insight
and enthusiasm.

Some specialist south of France/Côte d'Azur guides:
The Companion Guide to the South of France, Archibald Lyall, Collins.
Revised and expanded by A.N. Branagham (1978 edition reprinted).
A bit elderly as a guide, but truly a companion, written with love, amusement and knowledge. Excellent on artistic matters.
French Riviera/Côte d'Azur, Michelin Green Guide.
This indispensable guide provides hard information together with cultural and scenic value judgements delivered by way of the famous Michelin star system.
The South of France by John Ardagh, American Express/Mitchell Beazley (1983).
Handy slim format, small print, very full, by experienced and sympathetic writer. Some minor details slipping out of date.
A Touch of Monaco and the French Riviera Guide, pub. privately, UK distributor Lascelles Ltd, 47 York Road, Brentford, Middlesex TW8 0QP (1986).
Lively and chatty little work by local English-language journalists. Lots of good ideas.
The South of France, an Anthology, compiled by Laura Raison, Cadogan Publications.
Fine medley of literary observations and personal accounts of South of France over the centuries.

Health Regulations

There are no special health requirements or regulations for visitors to the Riviera.

Holidays (Public and Religious)

New Year's Day: 1 January
Easter Monday: variable
Labour Day: 1 May
VE Day: 8 May
Ascension Day: variable; sixth Thursday after Easter
Whitsun: variable; second Monday after Ascension
Bastille Day: 14 July
Assumption Day: 15 August
All Saints Day: 1 November
Remembrance Day: 11 November
Christmas Day: 25 December

Lost Property

Report serious losses — passport, credit cards, etc — to the police. For lost passports, inform the consulate, who will be able to issue emergency documents (see **Embassies and Consulates**, above). Loss of credit cards must be reported immediately to issuing company. Travellers' cheques are issued with instructions regarding loss (keep cheques separate from record of cheque numbers). Consulates may be able to help with emergency funds if travellers' cheques are lost or stolen. Hotels provide safe-keeping for valuables. If these are carried by the owner, take great care in crowded places. Restaurants, etc, are often helpful and honest in keeping lost articles.

Money Matters

The monetary unit is the franc; 100 centimes make one franc. There are coins of 10, 20 and 50 centimes, one franc, two francs, five francs and 10 francs. A new and smaller 10-franc piece is now in circulation alongside the older coin; many automatic

DIRECTORY

vending machines/parking ticket machines, etc are not yet adjusted for the new coin. Paper money for larger denominations. Banks, many of them state-owned, are the best place to change money, though service can be grudging. Most have exchange desks. Normal. opening hours 9 to noon, 14.00 to 16.00 weekdays, closed either Saturdays or Mondays. Closed Sundays and public holidays, and often on the intervening business day of a long weekend or *pont* – a bridge – where the public holiday falls on a Tuesday or Thursday. Hotels will change money but at lower rates. Credit cards, notably American Express, Carte Bleue (Visa/Barclaycard), Diners Club and Eurocard (Mastercard/Access), are willingly accepted by hotels, restaurants and the classier shops (but not in hypermarkets), and in many petrol stations.
Unlimited currency may be taken into France, but must be declared if bank notes to the value of Ff12,000 or more are likely to be re-exported.

Opening Times

Shopping Small shops usually 09.00 or 10.00 to noon or 12.30, then a long lunch hour; afternoon 14.30 to 19.00 or so. Afternoon opening in summer is often later, say from 16.00 to 20.00 or 21.00. Large shops – department stores, hyper-markets – usually 10.00 to 19.00, sometimes 20.00 on Friday. Some shops are closed on Mondays, others on Saturdays. **Banks** see **Money Matters,** above.

Museums Opening hours are brief and you are quite likely to arrive at a museum and find it shut. The system seems guaranteed to provoke frustration. Broadly, all national museums or national historic monuments administered from Paris close on Tuesdays. Many municipal museums close on Mondays, some on Thursdays, etc. Private galleries/museums, etc, close when they feel like it, which may be Sunday and Monday, or Thursday, etc. Many close for a month or so in November and the first half of December; others early in the New Year. Customary hours of opening are longer in summer, shorter in winter. Summer, typically: 10.00 to noon or 12.30, afternoon 14.30 to 18.30; winter, 10.00 to noon, afternoon 14.00 to 17.00.
Post Office hours see **Post Office,** below.

Personal Safety

The south of France offers no specific hazards other than sun-burn and twisting roads. These are often at a high level but they are generally well-maintained.

Pharmacist

Recognisable by the pharmacy's green cross, French pharmacists take an active role in medical care, usually offering both first aid and/or medical advice. Personnel are highly qualified and are able to prescribe and provide a range of drugs (though some are available only by prescription – *ordonnance*). Holiday and all night services *(pharmacie de garde)* are organised by rota, advertised on pharmacy doors, in local

Vence follows the pattern of many Riviera towns, retaining its own character despite rapid growth

newspapers and available from police stations. Pharmacie Principale, 10 rue Masséna, Nice (tel: 93 87 85 48) is also open all night.

Places of Worship
All towns and villages have Catholic churches. In Nice, Menton and St Raphael there are also churches offering English-language Anglican services: Holy Trinity Anglo-American Church, 11 rue Buffa, Nice St John, ave Carnot, Menton St John the Evangelist, ave Paul-Doumer, St Raphael.
Synagogues
7 rue Gustave-Deloyé, Nice 1 rue Boissy-d'Anglais, Nice

Police
The *Police Municipale* (blue uniforms) carry out normal police functions in the towns and cities. The *Gendarmes* (blue trousers, black jackets, white belts) are a national police force, covering the countryside and smaller places. The daunting CRS or *Compagnies Républicaines de Sécurité* handle emergencies, riots, etc, and also appear in milder form as guardians of safety on public beaches. The *Garde Mobile/Police de la Route* are the highway police. Monaco has its own special police force, very thick on the ground.

Post Office
All postal and telephone services are a government monopoly, the PTT or *Poste et Télécommunications*. Normal opening hours for main post offices are 08.00 to 19.00 weekdays, 08.00 to noon Saturdays, though small offices may close for lunch. Telexes may be sent from most main post offices, telegrams from post offices and via any subscriber-phone, *eg* hotel or friend's (dial 36 35). Some computerised information services may also

be available. Stamps are sold in post offices but may also be bought in tobacco shops (*tabacs*) or cafés marked with a red cigar sign. Letter boxes (*boîtes aux lettres*) are yellow.

Postal numbers Each Department of France has its own number, modifying for individual towns. In addressing a letter, the number should be placed before the name of the town. The two Departments covered in this guide are Alpes-Maritimes (number 06000) and Var (number 83000).

Poste restante Mail can be sent to you, and collected for a small charge, at any main post office. Address letters as follows: name, Poste Restante, Poste Centrale, Town's name (preceded by postal number), France.

See also **Telephones,** below.

Senior Citizens

The heat and somewhat frenetic activity of the Riviera in summer may or may not be an attraction; but the comparative calm and generally mild winter climate make it a fine place for relaxation, with plenty of opportunity for entertainment, cultural visits and strolling in the sunshine. A number of tour companies offer special arrangements for senior citizens (for further information contact Tourist Offices, whose addresses are given below).

Student and Youth Travel

For youth hostels, contact the National Youth Hostel Association or Fédération Unie des Auberges de Jeunesse, 6 rue Mesnil, 75116 Paris (tel: (1) 42 61 84 03). For special youth cards enabling the holder to eat at universities, for example, or obtain reductions at museums, ask in Tourist Offices in France (for addresses see **Tourist Offices**, below).

Telephones

French telephones are simple and unthreatening. All subscribers have an eight-figure number, a system which does away with dialling codes inside France — except for Paris. If dialling out of Paris to the provinces, add 16 before the eight-figure number; if dialling into Paris, add 16 (1) before the eight-figure number.

International dialling Into France, dial the international code, followed by 33 followed by the eight-figure number for the provinces. For Paris, dial the international code, then 33-1, then the number.

For international calls out of France, dial 19, wait for a new tone, then dial the national code, followed by the local code, omitting the initial 0 (zero), and then the number.

Call boxes May be coin or card. Cards on sale in post offices and as advertised on telephone booths, 50 or 120 units. After inserting the card, you have to close the flap over it before you can dial.

Telephone numbers For medical assistance, etc, see **Emergency Numbers,** above. For tourist information, see **Tourist Offices,** below.

Time (Local)

France follows Greenwich Mean Time plus one hour, with clocks put forward a further hour from late March to late September.

Tipping

Hotels, restaurants and cafés almost always include service on bills (service compris) but it is customary in restaurants to leave small change so as to round up the total; likewise at petrol stations. Do tip hotel porters, hotel maids, taxi drivers and hairdressers, on the same scale as at home.

Toilets

Dames for women; Messieurs or Hommes for men. May be standard toilet with seat or, in cafés, etc, may involve footrests and squatting. Self-cleansing toilets in fluted concrete are coming in fast in Nice and are very welcome but sometimes in architecturally inappropriate spots. If you are obliged to use a café toilet for lack of public facilities, perhaps order a coffee as a sign of good will. Coins on a dish and a lady peering at you suggest, of course, that a small contribution would be in order.

Tourist Offices

The French Government maintains a string of useful and friendly offices abroad. They possess a great deal of information and make a good starting point in planning any holiday in France.
In Britain: The French Government Tourist Office, 178 Piccadilly, London W1V 0AL (tel: 01-499 6911).
In Canada: 1981 Avenue McGill College, Montréal, Québec, H3A 2W9 (tel: 514 931 3855); 1 Dundas Street West, Suite 2405, Box 8, Toronto, Ontario, M5G 1Z3 (tel: 416 593 4717).
In USA: 610 Fifth Avenue, New York NY 10020 (tel: 212 757

The timeless charm of the Romans' 'province', or Provence, is a world away from the wealth and glamour of the Riviera's resorts

1125); 645 North Michigan Avenue, Chicago, Ill 60611 (tel: 312 337 6301); 9401 Wilshire Boulevard, Suite 314, Beverley Hills, CA 90212 (tel: 213 272 2661).
Once in France, there is an effective information network – through the larger Offices de Tourisme and the smaller Syndicats d'Initiative. All possess masses of information, usually in leaflet form, ranging from hotels and entertainment to

street maps and explanations of public transport. They are marked with the italic *i* (information) sign. Some can book hotels for you but are not allowed to make value judgements between one hotel and another. There is a minimal payment to cover their costs, telex, etc. Monaco has its own very efficient service.

Nice: Office de Tourisme, ave Thiers (tel: 93 87 07 07), left on exit from railway station; also Syndicat d'Initiative, 5 ave Gustave V (tel: 93 87 60 60); and at Nice-Parking on the way in from the airport (tel: 93 83 32 64).

Monaco: Direction du Tourisme et des Congrès, 2a boulevard des Moulins (tel: 93 30 87 01).

Cannes: Office de Tourisme, Palais des Festivals, Esplanade Président Georges Pompidou, La Croisette (tel: 93 39 24 53); also at railway station (tel: 93 99 19 77).

St Tropez: Maison du Tourisme, 23 ave Général Leclerc (tel: 94 97 41 21).

Almost all the smaller towns also have their own information offices.

LANGUAGE

English is widely understood in this extremely cosmopolitan area. However, attempts to speak French are appreciated in simpler surroundings, and, naturally enough, the more one speaks, the more one understands. There are many simple phrase books and guides to language, and travelling with one of these to hand is recommended.

Here are just one or two words which may be helpful:

Yes Oui
No Non
Good morning Bonjour
Good afternoon/evening/night Bonsoir
Please S'il vous-plaît
Thank you Merci/merci beaucoup
Sorry Pardon

Numbers

One un/une
two deux
three trois
four quatre
five cinq
six six
seven sept
eight huit
nine neuf
ten dix
eleven onze
twelve douze
twenty vingt
fifty cinquante
one hundred cent
one thousand mille

Days of the Week

Monday lundi
Tuesday mardi
Wednesday mercredi
Thursday jeudi
Friday vendredi
Saturday samedi
Sunday dimanche

Months

January janvier
February février
March mars
April avril
May mai
June juin
July juillet
August août
September septembre
October octobre
November novembre
December décembre